THE
FIVE-MINUTE
ILIAD
and Other
Instant Classics
Great Books for the Short Attention Span

Greg Nagan

Illustrated by Tony Millionaire

A Fireside Book
Published by Simon & Schuster
New York   London   Toronto   Sydney   Singapore

For everyone who has ever been forced to read *Beowulf.*
For my children, without whom I was able to write it.
(I have no children.)
And for my parents, Anne and Doug.

FIRESIDE
Rockefeller Center
1230 Avenue of the Americas
New York, NY 10020

Designed by Diane Hobbing /Snap-Haus Graphics

Manufactured in the United States of America
10   9   8   7   6   5   4   3   2   1
Library of Congress Cataloging-in-Publication Data
Nagan, Greg.
    The five-minute Iliad and other instant classics : great books for the short
attention span / Greg Nagan ; illustrated by Tony Millionaire.
        p. cm.
    1. Parodies. 2. Canon (Literature)—Humor. I. Title.
    PN6231.P3 N34 2000
    818'.5407—dc21
                                                                00-022750

ISBN 0-684-86767-2

"The Five-Minute *Iliad*" was originally broadcast on *A Prairie Home Companion* on October 12, 1996, in a somewhat different form.

Contents

I will never write such wordy trash again.
—Count Leo Tolstoy, on *War and Peace*

Author's Introduction:
Why Read the Great Books?

"The unexamined life isn't worth living," Plato said. Scholars like to quote that line, but they neglect to mention that the remark was addressed to a buxom young urologist named Bubbles.

The unexamined life is pretty sweet. Let's face it: not many of us could stand up to the scrutiny of a dozen cable and broadcast news network reporters camped out in our front yards—let alone actual journalists. As the ancient Sumerian proverb has it, "I don't have a drinking problem. I drink. I get drunk. I fall down. No problem."

Alas for the Sumerians!

(The dwindling attention span is another question worthy of consideration.)

On the other hand, if you don't familiarize yourself with the themes and ideas of the Great Books, you're going to lead a miserable life and die. You'll probably lead a miserable life and die anyway, but an acquaintance with the Great Books can help you understand your misery and death in a broader context. That's got to count for something.

Familiarity with the Great Books can also help you impress people.

"But why should I worry about impressing anyone?" you ask. (If it wasn't you, it was someone who looked like you.) I'll tell you: it is my hypothesis that we have all been put on this wretched rock expressly to impress one another.

Maybe your boss would be more inclined to raise your salary

if he or she thought you were conversant with Renaissance literature. Maybe your teacher would give you higher grades if you peppered your papers with allusions to Homeric mythology. Maybe you have to give a speech, and want to make sure your audience knows you're smarter than they are. Maybe you're running for public office in the greater Boston area. Or maybe you're just one of the millions of adults trying to get into an English major's pants.

Whatever the reason, sooner or later you're going to have to impress someone, and I have therefore unselfishly prepared this book for your edification.

Exculpatory Remarks (Excuses)

The overwhelming majority of the texts included in this book were written by white European males, almost all of whom are dead. This is not my fault. I did not kill any of the authors (which is not to say I wouldn't have, had the opportunity presented itself), and I did not decide what books ought to survive the forced march of history. I therefore smugly absolve myself of all responsibility for the unequal distribution of genders, cultures, geographies, sexual preferences, and hat sizes represented herein. The books I chose are all indisputable Western classics. Harold Bloom says so.

Also, because I couldn't include all the classics, I had to omit some. That's just how it is. Like everything else, this is not my fault. I will only observe that I have deliberately omitted the great humorists, such as Cervantes, Fielding, Voltaire, Swift, and Twain, because humor is vulgar and has no place in literature.

Lastly, I have tried to maintain the strictest possible academic standards for this book, in the hopes that it might be mistaken for a scholarly work. I have therefore included several footnotes. Unfortunately, I didn't have time to consult any authoritative texts, so at the time this book went to press the sources cited did not yet exist. It is my sincere hope that by the time this book appears in stores, they will.

The Five-Minute History
of Western Civ

Thousands of years ago, a bunch of people got together around the Tigris and Euphrates rivers and decided they would start Western Civilization, largely because they had no television or diet cola. Although the eventual emergence of infomercials would lead some to conclude otherwise, it has generally been agreed since that long-ago day that Western Civilization was, indeed, a good idea.

It took some time to get things going, because there was an awful lot of cleaning to do, but eventually they got around to inventing Western literature. The first subjects to be treated in Western literature were rocks, trees, and weather, since that was all there was. As time went by, however, Western Civilization began to exhibit symptoms of History, Politics, Religion, and Sex, and this resulted in more interesting literature.

The oldest surviving works of Western literature are the Bible and the *Epic of Gilgamesh*. Both books were popular best-sellers, and they fought bitterly for the number one spot on the charts. It was a fierce struggle, as there was only one chart and they were the only books on it. Eventually the Bible won out. *Gilgamesh* partisans were outraged, and withdrew from Western Civilization.

Meanwhile, Greek civilization had arisen and imbued Western Civilization with some of its core values, notably Democracy, Philosophy, and Moussaka. Eventually Greek civilization was traded in for the Roman empire, which didn't offer as much Democracy, Philosophy, or Eggplant, but did have more orgies.

In the middle of the Roman empire, a carpenter's son from the town of Galilee in Judaea began teaching people not to throw stones at each other. The Romans disapproved, and he was therefore crucified. This resulted in Christianity, which gradually became the Official Religion of Western Civilization.

Upon the fall of Rome, which most historians attribute to the difficulty of learning Latin, Western Civilization slowed down for a few hundred years while people tried to invent an easier language. This led to considerable disagreement, and therefore caused Countries. In the midst of this confusion, Big Scary Monsters saw their opportunity and attacked. The Great Writers knew a good story when they saw one, and many of them wrote about the Big Scary Monsters even though their languages weren't done yet.

Another thing that happened to Western Civilization during this period was the discovery of the first completely Christian country, Hell. As with a previous great discovery of Western Civilization, THE LAW, people no sooner became aware of it than they began trying to figure ways to avoid it. The Great Writers exploited this opportunity and wrote at length about Hell: what it was like, who lived there, how richly they deserved to suffer and burn, and how it was therefore probably a good idea not to be wicked. (Wickedness itself was held to be synonymous with deviance from the Great Writers' point of view.)

Efforts to develop a new language were still under way, but one particular group of people (the Infidels) went too far and invented a new religion. They were therefore kicked out of Western Civilization, and people organized expeditions to track them down and kill them. These expeditions were called the Crusades, and although they were one of Western Civilization's first Very Bad Ideas, the Great Writers experienced great success writing about them, and Western literature was the richer for it.

After all the excitement of the Big Scary Monsters, Hell, and the Crusades, things slowed down for a while and Western Civilization became bored. Whole centuries passed while people tried to think of something to do. Finally they decided to chuck it all and start from scratch, resulting in the Renaissance, which was a Very Good Idea.

Things picked up a little during the Renaissance, and they had a Reformation to make it even more interesting. This included a Diet of Worms, which drove some people to flee Western Civilization altogether. Unfortunately they discovered the New World, which turned out to be just another part of

Western Civilization. All of this resulted in the Age of Exploration and the Era of Imperialist Colonialism, which were frowned on by indigenous peoples, many of whom refused to join Western Civilization until they had been eliminated, at which point they embraced it.

By now the English language was almost ready, and Shakespeare was invented in order that the British would have someone impressive to quote. There were many Shakespeares, to the extent that the only British citizen whom we can safely presume not to have been William Shakespeare was William Shakespeare. As soon as English had been perfected and Britain had colonized the world, they invented British literature to reinforce their status as Best Country. This was the Golden Age of British Screenwriting.

Outside Britain it was generally considered unfair that Britain had become Best Country. Nowhere was this more keenly felt than in France, where they had invented their own language ("French," or, in English, "English"), and had accumulated numerous remarkable achievements of their own, such as the French Revolution, Napoleon, the Louvre, soft cheese, etc. They felt slighted, as did the Spanish, the Portuguese, the Dutch, the Austrians, and the Poles. (The Germans and Italians also felt slighted, but they had not yet invented their own countries, and were therefore discouraged from complaining.)

Indeed, by now there were scores of countries, all of whom felt they deserved to be Best Country. The competition was fierce, and often led to War. Many countries thought they'd have a better shot of being Best Country if they had better leaders, so there were also a lot of revolutions.

The most famous of these was the Industrial Revolution. The growth of Industry meant that fewer people had to work on farms, and more people could live in the city. It also improved the Economy, which meant more people could get drunk.

It was a terrible, bloody, drunken, and confusing period, and therefore caused the Modern Age.

• • •

From the end of the nineteenth into the dawn of the twentieth century, Western Civilization had a lot of wars to try and settle the question of who was Best Country once and for all. Most of these proved inconclusive. In and around the time of the First World War, a lot of Great Writers from every country went to Paris and got drunk. (Paris was chosen because it was so accessible, as the Germans had repeatedly proven.) The Tourists—or, as they preferred to be called, the Expatriates—were almost constantly drunk, but one night when they were sober they made one of Western Civilization's greatest discoveries: that War was a Bad Idea. This revelation astonished the world.

In the decades that followed, a lot of Great Writers looked around Western Civilization and all the fighting over who was Best Country, and decided that, whoever ended up winning, Western Civilization was doomed. To prove it, they wrote books about futures in which the wrong country had become Best Country, and how awful life would be in such a world. These books opened people's eyes, and Western Civilization was therefore saved at the expense of making these Great Writers look very silly.

Meanwhile, however, no one was really sure who had become Best Country. The only thing people knew for sure was that it definitely wasn't Germany, and this made the Germans very mad (they were almost always mad anyway, since they had to speak that awful language and wear lederhosen). And so the Germans decided to have another World War, which very nearly resulted in the end of Western Civilization. It also led to America's developing the Biggest Bomb, which automatically resulted in its becoming Best Country.

The only people who disagreed were the Russians, who were no longer Russians but Soviets, and therefore bad. They had also developed Big Bombs, although not quite as big. The United States and the Soviets squared off, and every country in the world was forced to pick sides. Eventually the United States succeeded in building a McDonald's in Red Square, and the Soviets conceded defeat.

At the end of the twentieth century, Western Civilization finally invented the computer and the Internet, which made it much easier to get pictures of naked people. This was bad for Western literature, which had of course succeeded in the past largely as an alternative to looking at naked people. (For pictures of naked people, see Appendix A, "Pictures of Naked People.")

The Iliad

by Homer

(700 B.C.)

No, my friend,
I have no desire to fight the blithe immortals.
But if you're a man who eats the crops of the earth,
a mortal born for death—here, come closer,
the sooner you will meet your day to die!

Homer (no relation) was a blind poet who lived in Greece around the ninth or eighth century B.C., and, as a result of the curious Greek dating system, was apparently born about eighty years after he died. It is believed the Iliad *and the* Odyssey, *his two surviving works, were both originally oral rather than written works, which goes a long way toward explaining how a blind guy could have written them thousands of years before the invention of Braille. The* Iliad *is a vital piece of literature for all readers, because all the greatest writers of Western Civilization have been alluding to it for eons ("alluding to" being Greek for "stealing from"). This is an abridged translation, meaning I have skipped all those parts of the epic that might have been troublesome to translate and have made up the rest. Also, it does not rhyme and has no meter. I assure the reader that in all other regards this is almost a faithful presentation of the* Iliad.*

Ancient Greek civilization flowered around 500 B.C.,[1] *at which point it became classic. Its eventual decline was the result of ouzo and philosophy, which might have been survived separately, but taken together proved too much.*

Rage—Goddess, sing the rage of Peleus' son Achilles!
If you don't know it I can hum a few bars.
Murderous, doomed, he cost the Achaeans countless losses
(or the Argives, or the Greeks, same difference),
hurling down to the House of Death so many sturdy souls
that they opened an Achilles wing. And gave a discount.
Begin, Muse, when the two got in each other's faces,
Agamemnon lord of men and brilliant Achilles.

[1]See footnote in *The Inferno.*

What god drove them to fight with such a fury?
Apollo the son of Zeus and Leto. Why? Who knows.
The gods have reasons, and see things unseen by us,
their wisdom penetrates all mysteries;
and also, they can be pissy.

And so Apollo, God of the sun,
Golden-faced Apollo, did drive a wedge between them,
Agamemnon and Achilles, general and warrior, friend and
    friend.
And so the warrior Achilles, great Achilles, was moved to
    anger
and would not lead his men to fight beside Agamemnon
unless Agamemnon said he was sorry, and begged forgiveness,
and didn't just say it, but really meant it.
But that lord of men, that Agamemnon, was proud,
and would not say he was sorry, because he wasn't,
and why should he apologize anyway? Wasn't he general?
Didn't anyone know how hard it was to be general?
Didn't anyone care about *his* feelings?

And so while the Greeks, or Achaeans, or Argives,
or some combination thereof, but not necessarily limited
    thereto,
laid siege to Troy, or Ilium, that impenetrable city,
whose walls rose from the plain like something really tall
    and flat
rising out of something really broad and flat,
as they laid siege, Achilles and his men hung back,
sat around on their ships, bided their time, got drunk,
and played quarters. And without them
Agamemnon's force was weak, and Troy beheld this,
and Hector, noble Hector, valiant Hector, son of Priam,
saw this too, and thought, "Woo-hoo!"

Out came the Trojans! Led by mighty Hector
out of their walled city, out against Agamemnon,
and they started to kick some fanny.

How many Greeks fell at that time? How many stout heroes
did the valiant Trojan arms dispatch?
Lots.

For example Gingivitis, son of Halitosis,
Gingivitis the flaxen-haired, the glinty-eyed,
how he howled his song of death
as the Trojan speartip penetrated first the epidermis,
breaking the skin, then pressed on through tissue,
severing sinew and tendon alike, glancing off the sternum,
then into the aorta, puncturing that valve,
glutting up the aortal cavity, resulting in cardiac arrest
and death. And not just that flaxen-haired youth, but many
        others too,
their flesh was scattered about the field, they died in droves,
it was a really bad scene. Agamemnon ordered the retreat,
and the Trojans took a breather.

So Agamemnon called to him Odysseus, wily Odysseus,
whom you probably know better as Ulysses,
even though they're the same guy. Odysseus was Achilles'
        friend.
Agamemnon knew this. He told wily Ulysses to get
        Achilles,
and Odysseus said he would.

And so Odysseus went to Achilles. He met him in his tent.
Ulysses was wily, and full of guile,
and therefore didn't get right to the point
but shot the breeze a little, chewed the fat,

and tried to get Achilles feeling comfortable.
And finally he told him why he'd come,
told him of the Argive losses, and the Greek,
and the Achaean (he was just as confused as anyone else),
and how Agamemnon had sent him,
and how even though he hadn't actually said he was sorry,
Ulysses could swear Agamemnon *looked* sorry,
and wasn't that enough?

And Achilles said unto him, "What are you, high?"

And so Odysseus went back to Agamemnon,
who bade him tell all Achilles had said.
Agamemnon lord of men heard all, and it hurt his feelings,
and he said Achilles was a heel.

Rosy-fingered Dawn then brought another day: more
     fighting,
more Trojan victories, more dead Greeks, Achaeans, and
     Argives.
It was really bad and Agamemnon didn't know what to do.
So he retreated again. And sent another guy to Achilles.
Phoenix, this time. Old Phoenix, wise Phoenix,
Phoenix with arthritis he wouldn't wish on a dog.

Phoenix went to Achilles and talked about the weather,
and his bunions, and his digestion, and how it wasn't the heat,
it was the humidity. And Achilles said,
"Go back to Agamemnon, your general Agamemnon,
and tell him he can blow it out his ass."
And old Phoenix did go back, cursing and muttering,
     incensed!
To think: that an old soldier should come to this!,
it wasn't how they'd done things in his day!,

and on and on like that, the way an old guy gets
when some young guy pisses him off.

And Agamemnon heard the message,
and now he was really angry. And he could hardly wait
for rosy-fingered Dawn to come along again,
but at last she did, and it was another day, another battle.
The Trojans pressed hard, and more Achaeans died,
and more Argives, and now Hector had led his men down,
down to the Achaean ships,
and had the Greek army pressed against the shore
and was pretty sure it was a done deal
but called it a night anyway
figuring he could mop up the next day.

Now, Achilles had a friend, Patroclus, his best friend:
they'd grown up together, they were homies.
And Patroclus came to Achilles that night,
and told him he was sure they were going to lose,
they were all going to die,
unless Achilles got over himself and brought his men
to join Agamemnon's army and kick some Trojan booty.

Achilles loved Patroclus—not like that,
but you know, the way guys love each other—
and he didn't want Patroclus to die,
so he told him: "Listen. Take my armor. Take my men.
Fight the Trojans, kick their butts. But I won't fight,
I can't fight, until Agamemnon says he's sorry—
and he can't just say it, he has to really mean it."
And Patroclus was like, "Okay, cool."
And Achilles said, "One more thing:
don't mess with Hector. I mean it."
And Patroclus was all, *whatever.*

Early the next day, once rosy-fingered Dawn arose,
how it heartened the embattled Argives
to see Achilles' men join them in the fray!
With great gladness now they poured forth,
and beat the Trojans back, and chopped them into little
    pieces,
little bitty pieces, that made nasty squishy noises when you
    stepped on them,
so you tried not to step on them, only you couldn't help it,
they were everywhere, little julienned strips of Trojans,
an eyeball here, a kneecap there, clumps of hair and gristle,
floppy flaps of flesh, and splintered bone, and pools of
    blood.
And at the head of the Argive ranks, brave Patroclus!
Achilles' friend Patroclus! Patroclus whom Achilles loved—
not like that, not really, although, yeah, they'd experimented
    in puberty,
but neither of them really liked it, and it was just part of
    growing up,
those feelings were perfectly natural, all part of being
    human—
Patroclus was killing Trojans left and right, and right and
    left,
he forged a trail of death through the Trojan ranks,
until he saw Hector, noble Hector, and remembered
    Achilles' words.

Zeus above, high in the vault of heaven, eyes of Olympus,
your will determines all, even from way the heck up there.
And so you willed it that Patroclus, greathearted Patroclus,
extremely excitable Patroclus, should in his fury forsake
the warning from his special friend.

He threw his spear at Hector:
wide right. Another: wide left. And Hector saw him there,

saw Patroclus standing in Achilles' armor,
and therefore thought he *was* Achilles,
since he didn't know about the whole armor loan deal,
which could have made for a funny bunch of mix-ups
in another sort of story. But in this one, it was harsh:
Hector killed Patroclus. One spear, one corpse.
Bada bing.

And Hector took the armor off Patroclus,
and wore it himself, and danced around the corpse
of the mighty fallen hero. And you can just imagine
the rollicking high jinks that might still have ensued
if this were a play by, oh—say, Noël Coward.

At the end of the day they gave Achilles the news:
his friend was slain at Hector's hand.
He didn't take it well. He had loved Patroclus—
not like that, but you know—no! He *had* loved him like
    that!
He didn't care who knew! He loved him, and he would
    avenge him.
Impatient Achilles didn't even wait for Dawn, rosy-fingered
    bitch,
but he put on his armor, Achilles did—
not his good armor, which he had given to Patroclus,
which had caused the whole misunderstanding in the first
    place—
but his other armor, the spare set,
that he always brought in case of emergency.

And out he went and threw himself against the Trojan lists.
They hadn't been expecting anyone at that hour,
so he was able to whale on them pretty good for a while.
And even when the element of surprise wore off,
such was the wrath of Achilles, such his rage,

such his general cantankerous furor,
that he sliced through the Trojan ranks
like something hard and sharp through something really
    soft
until at last he beheld his nemesis, assassin of his friend,
Hector, prince of Troy.

Achilles' eyes flashed with thunder, he roared out lightning
    rage:
"I swear to Zeus I'll kill you, Hector, to avenge my special
    friend!"
And Hector, mighty Hector, just smiled and raised his spear.
"You shouldn't swear to Zeus, you fool—not so near your
    end!"

Hey, that rhymed.

So valiant Hector loosed his spear, and it whistled o'er the
    bloody field
(not any particular tune, but a general sort of whistle,
the kind created from a projectile vibrating through the air),
and wide it flew, a mile wide, and Achilles laughed out loud.
"Missed me!" cried the raging hero, "Missed me!
Now ya gotta kiss me!"

Undaunted Hector drew again, aimed a second spear.
Achilles crouched, prepared to dodge—and here it comes!
    He leaps!
Wide left! No good! Now Hector stands unspeared!
He draws his sword and rushes forth, prepared to slay
    Achilles;
that hero holds his spear aloft, eyes afire, taking aim.
But wait! Behold! Isn't that his armor?
When it comes to irony, the gods can sure deliver. Like
    Domino's.

Achilles knew his armor well, knew its impervious mettle.
He knew he couldn't pierce its hardness.
So as Hector came toward him, his terrible sword raised
    high,
Achilles aimed for the neck and threw—and hit!
And the spear plunged through the skin,
and punctured the larynx, and shattered the vertebrae,
and severed the spinal cord. So much for Hector.
And Achilles took his corpse and tied it to his chariot,
then rode around the walls of Troy, dragging Hector in the
    dust,
and did doughnuts.

And that was pretty much that.

And old King Priam, Hector's father,
had to beg Achilles for the body of his noble son
so he could bury it, and honor it, and do whatever it was
that old men did with their dead sons' bodies.
And Hecuba cried, but what is she to you? What are you to
    her?
Or however that goes.

Anyway, the main thing is: great Hector was dead,
and they buried him. And Achilles was doomed
because of this prophecy that I forgot to mention
from the oracle at Delphi, which had foretold that
not long after Hector's death, Achilles too would perish,
so it's not like he could celebrate.

Also, when Agamemnon finally got home his wife killed
    him.
Then his son Orestes killed her, his own mother,
and then the Furies hounded him for vengeance.
It was this whole big tragedy.

And most of the Trojan woman had to whore themselves, or
worse.

And it took Ulysses twenty years to sail home to Ithaca
because he was a great proud man and would not ask for
directions.
And when he finally did get home, his dog died.

So it was pretty much a bummer
all the way around.

—The End—

The Divine Comedy: Part I, Inferno

by Dante Alighieri

(1315)

If thou art, Reader, slow now to believe
what I shall say, it will no marvel be,
for I who saw it hardly can admit it . . .

Dante Alighieri was born in Florence, Italy, nearly two centuries before any of the other great explorers, but in about A.D.[1] *1300 he made one of the most significant discoveries of Western Civilization. He discovered and charted the first purely Christian country: Hell.*

Dante is known by his first name, like other geniuses of the early Italian Renaissance, such as Michelangelo and Elvis. He was a popular poet in his native Florence. The various kingdoms (which were not all kingdoms) of Italy (which was not Italy) at that time were in constant conflict (which was sometimes peaceful). There were Guelphs and Ghibellines, Whites and Blacks, and an abundance of Evil Bastards. Dante enjoyed the art of Italian politics, and he was eventually exiled from Florence for being a White Rook during an invasion of Black Bishops.

There are three parts to The Divine Comedy: Inferno, *Purgatorio, and* Paradiso. *Dante died before he could finish the fourth part,* Spaghettio.

Everyone who translates Inferno *gets to draw a picture of it. Here's mine:*

[1]A.D. stands for the Latin *Anno Domini,* meaning "After Dinner," from the early Christian habit of dating on the basis of years elapsed since they'd had their last good meal. (For most of the church fathers, this was of course the Last Supper, even though Judas had spoiled it with all his treachery, etc.) B.C., by contrast, stands for "Backward Counting." Many modern scholars prefer to use C.E. and B.C.E. See Dr. Whoopenkauff's engaging article on dating conventions ("Things That Piss Me Off") in the March 1998 edition of *Jack and Jill* magazine.

Dante wrote Inferno *in colloquial Italian. (Colloquial for "collo-quial," for example, would be "the way normal people talk.") The best-known English translation is Henry Wadsworth Longfellow's, which uses words like* hence *and* thence *and* wherefore, *and* thee *and* thou *and* thither. *This is not colloquial, and therefore Bad. So I have translated Mr. Longfellow's translation.*

Dante invented the "terza rima" form of verse for his Divine Comedy. *The terza rima consists of three lines, where the middle line of each triplet rhymes with the first and last lines of the next triplet. Following the example of my English translation predecessors, I have ignored this formula completely. Instead of terza rima, which is complex and Italian, I have chosen the verse form best known to most Americans: the limerick. And where it was hard to rhyme, I made up words.*

Canto I[2]

In the midst of my summer vacation
I suffered disorientation
    in the woods I got lost
    while a strong tempest tossed
and I thought to myself, "Well, damnation!"

At the foot of a mountain I stood
and I wondered if climb it I should
    but my internal banter
    was cut short by a panther
whose intentions did not appear good.

---

[2] *The Divine Comedy* has 100 cantos, pretty evenly divided between its three parts. To help the modern reader cope with Dante, I have translated the entire *Inferno* into one canto. No other translation does this.

As bad as things looked, they got worse,
as if it were some kind of curse:
    a lion appeared,
      then a wolf, and I feared
my demise would be somewhat perverse.[3]

It was then that a ghostly form flickered
and with these three beasts briefly bickered
    they ran off in fear
      of the ghost's ghastly sneer
(and I swear that I hadn't been liquored).

I ought to have let it all pass,
once he'd scared off those creatures *en masse,*
    but it only seemed right
      to be more polite
so I thanked him for saving my ass.

The ghost said, «I'm Virgil, the poet.
My name's not obscure, you should know it.
    I once made my home
      in the city of Rome,
I've been sent here to save you, don't blow it.»

I said, "You old guys are so freaking lame
to think everyone must know your names.
    And those dumb Euro-quotes
      don't improve anecdotes—
please use this kind, they work just the same."

---

[3]Scholars have debated the symbolic meaning of these three beasts for centuries. I prefer Professor Gerblich's hypothesis that the panther, lion, and wolf represent a panther, lion, and wolf (although not necessarily in that order). I am also intrigued, but remain unconvinced, by Sir Richard Furtooth's interpretation that they represent Brie, Camembert, and Gruyère.

Virgil said, "Never mind, listen well.
I can help you get through this ordell."
    He said with a grin,
     as he wiped off his chin,
"Come on, Dante, we're going to Hell."

You probably think it's amusing,
but to me it was only confusing
    that "helping me well"
     meant a trip down to Hell.
I thought, *What kind of drugs is he using?*

COME THROUGH ME TO THE SORROWFUL CITY.
COME THROUGH ME AND FORGET ABOUT PITY.
    EVERY LAST DOPE
     MUST ABANDON ALL HOPE
WHEN THEY PASS ON INTO ETERNITY.

When I read those grand words on the gate
I told Virgil I'd happily wait.
    He said, "Please be braver,
     it's only a waiver,
legalese mumbo-jumbo, not Fate."

The first circle's real dark and quiet
but billions of souls have to try it.
    It isn't the bimbos
     that end up in Limbo
But Unbaptized Heathens abide it.

The next circle echoed with groans
and was whirling with spirits high-flown.
    In life they chased Lusts,
     so now they chased gusts
(but at least they were still getting blown).

The subsequent circle didn't cheer us,
for none of its souls would come near us.
    The Gluttons all stuck
      in their miserable muck
and sometimes got chewed by Cerberus.

The fourth one was guarded by Plutus,
whose foulmouthed nonsense saluted us.
    The Spenders here fight
      the Hoarders each night
and each side did its best to recruit us.

The next circle had such a stink
that I didn't know what to think
    The Wrathful made trouble,
      the Mopey made bubbles
in steaming black marshes of skink.

Heretics were found in the sixth,
in quite an uncomfortable fixth.
    In open tombs toasted,
      like pizzas they roasted—
or candles, their heads being wicksth.

The next circle came in three parts:
one for each of the violent arts.
    First Homicidals,
      then Suicidals,
and lastly "Unnatural" hearts.

The first was a ring of red blood
as clotty and viscous as mud.
    The violenter sinners
      were deeper put inner:
armed centaurs stood by, chewing cud.

The Suicides turn into bushes
with branches where once they had tushes;
    their legs are all twigs
    between which grow sprigs,
and yet not a one of them blushes.

The last was a featureless plain
where a liquidy fire it rained
    we hung out a while
    to meet pedophiles
and my guide asked me wryly, "How's Beatrice?"

The eighth circle held those who lied,
from forger to fraud to tour guide.
    It was therefore split
    into ten separate pits
(its popularity can't be denied).

The first pouch resembled Times Square
full of trumpets and strumpets and snares
    around us meandering,
    seduction and pandering—
and demons who watched with great care.

In the next pouch I grew too aware
of a stench that I hardly could bear.
    The Flatterers float
    in a giant shit moat,
which proves flattery gets you *some*where.

Next came the pouch of Simoniacs
condemned to amend for their phony acts.
    The salvation they sold
    got them stuffed in dark holes
with their feet sticking outward, those holy hacks.

Diviners who'd misled the masses
were trapped in the fourth ring's morasses:
  their heads were turned round
  so that if they looked down
they were staring direct at their asses.

In the next pocket boiling in pitch,
Politicians who'd made themselves rich.
  They'd never wavered
  from selling their favors
but now watch those rat bastards twitch!

In the sixth pouch we found situated
Hypocrites who are forever fated
  never to talk
  but ever to walk
in cumbersome cloaks, iron-plated.

The next pouch was home to the Thieves
who had nothing left up their sleeves:
  for sleeves lose their charm
  when you haven't got arms
and as snakes that's the fate they receive.

We next to the eighth pocket came
where we met with some infamous names.
  In life they misled folks
  so now that they're dead folks
their egos are truly inflamed.

The Schismatics in the next pouchy
had reason enough to be grouchy:
  no longer quite whole,
  from head to asshole
they'd been split down the middle. That's ouchy.

The worst Falsifiers are found
in the tenth of the eighth circle's rounds.
    They rot and decay,
      their wounds leak away,
and in their own pus they all drown.

Betrayal has been judged the worst.
Among all the sins it ranks first.
    You can't make amends
      for screwing your friends:
to chilly Cocytus you're cursed.

Its four frozen rings here begin
with those who betrayed their own kin
    they're up to their heads
      in Caina's ice-bed,
and loudly express their chagrin.

Antenora's the next destination,
for betrayers of party or nation.
    They're stacked closer here
      and they chew on their peers
which I looked on with some fascination.

The next ring is called Ptolomea,
for those who their guests did betraya
    Their souls here abide
      before they have died
while demons go live out their daysa.

Of these rings Judecca's the last
for treachery most unsurpassed:
    they're trapped in the ice
      like the dots in clear dice—
but in their case the die's never cast.

At last here was Hell's center spot
which I'd always thought would be hot.
    It was surprising
      to see Satan rising
from the ice-bed in which he was caught.

Each of Satan's three mouths was employed
on the head of one grim treacheroid:
    Cassius, then Brutus,
      and in the third Judas.
They were more than a little annoyed.

Virgil wasn't a bad commentator,
no one could have led us through straighter.
    But when he said, "Come,
      we've only begun!"
I said, "Sorry, Virge. See you later."

—The End—

Notes on the film: *Irwin Allen's* The Towering Inferno *was criticized by many scholars for its too liberal interpretation of Dante's text, and these criticisms may have been responsible for the film's failure to achieve recognition by the Academy.*

Poem Advisory

The following chapter is in verse. The author realizes that the previous two chapters were also in verse. The author isn't any happier about it than you are. Readers who have had their fill of poetry are advised to advance to the nineteenth century (page 63), and to return to the Protestant Reformation at their leisure.

(Readers are advised against reading as far ahead as *Dracula* before returning, however, lest they find themselves going from bat to verse.)

Paradise Lost

by John Milton

(1667)

. . . To thee I call,
But with no friendly voice, and add thy name,
O Sun, to tell thee how I hate thy beams
That bring to my remembrance from what state
I fell, how glorious once above thy Spheare;
Till Pride and worse Ambition threw me down,
Warring in Heav'n against Heav'n's matchless King:
Ah wherefore!

In the sixteenth century Western Civilization was convulsed by the Reformation, which caused Protestants. This was an important development, as it allowed for much more religious persecution than had previously been possible. Over the next hundred years, Western Civilization became a bubbling cauldron of disparate religious denominations. One of the great theological debates of the age was whether heretics should be hanged, burned alive, or drawn and quartered.

John Milton was an Englishman in the seventeenth century who believed fervently in the Puritan Reformation. Sadly for Milton, but happily for England, the Puritan Reformation was soundly defeated, and the Puritans fled to America, which was as pure and incorruptible then as it is today. In all the confusion, poor John Milton got left behind, and like so many other fervent believers, he subsequently went blind and wrote an epic poem. And like so many other epic poets, he was in no mood to rhyme.

Paradise Lost was published in 1667, when Milton was fifty-nine years old. Many critics and theologians have had difficulty explaining Milton's brilliant and complex portrayal of Satan, who despite being the antagonist of the epic still seems to come off better than God or Jesus. These critics and theologians have overlooked the one inviolable truth of religion and screenwriting: good is boring.

A Note on the Verse

The measure is English Heroic Verse, without Rime, as that of Homer in Greek, and of Virgil in Latin, and of other writers in other divers Languages whose names escape me, I not having writ them down in my Notebooks as I ought to have, but rather on bits of Paper lying about the House, which Scraps I later scarce can find. It is without Rime because Rime is no necessary Adjunct or true Ornament of Poem or good Verse, but rather a Pain unto my Buttoks, as only Idiots are like to find Pleasure in Rime, and only Simpletons admire Rime, and unto Idiots and Simpletons alike I say Faugh! Faugh! Faugh!
—And again, Faugh!

Book I

Of Man's First Disobedience, and the Fruit
Of that Forbidden Tree, whose mortal tast
Brought Death into the World, of all our woe,
Sing Heav'nly Muse—Sing out loud, sing out strong,
Don't worry if it's not Good enow
For anyone else to hear—just sing, sing a song!
(But try to keep it short, if you don't mind.)
Sing of th'Infernal Satan, whose Rebel Rankes
Of Angels hath embattled God, defied Him,
Hath thought to o'erthrow th'Eternal Throne,
And make themselves Top Angels of Heav'n,
And (Big Surprise!) hath been whaled upon
By God, and vanquished by Him, and kicked hard
Upside their heads by Him, and knocked about
By furious faithful Cherubim, those little Snits,
Withal o'ercome in battel and sent down,
Out of th'ethereal air, down to the lake of Fyre,
Where for nine days and nine nights they lay,

Vanquished, wretched, groaning their incalculable Loss,
Wond'ring if maybe it hadn't been such a Good Idea,
Trying to get over on God.

High-perched, Satan surveyed their lot
And beheld his many damnèd peers.
Studlymanus, for example,
Who oft in Heav'n had combed his golden locks,
Bragging of the Angel Babes he'd bagged:
Now hornèd, feet cloven, with fangs and claws,
And dandruffe, and acne, and foule Breath;
His anguished cries roared out, unheard
By his thousand self-abhorring Peers.
Like Ganglyass, and Vulvatron,
Thus too even Puffles the Wanker:
A thousand thousand tortured cries
As each beheld the self-same fate:
Angels no more: they were all messed up.

With thundrous Voice did Satan boom
His Speech to his wretched fallyn rankes:
"Valiant fellow Soldiers! Warriors brave!
Knocked thus low we waken to our Station,
Defeated, cast down, engulfed in Flaymes,
But remember ye all, remember ye the Ant!
Recall ye what made that lyttle olde Ant
Bethink himself to move that Rubber Tree Plante!
He had high Hopes—hath we not high hopes?
Hath we not high, Apple Pye, in the Skye hopes?
All of ye, joine together, ev'ry one!"
And soon the flaming Pit resounded
With grim and groaning fiendish Chorus,
Singing along around the Fyre.

Book II

Then began Satan the Meeting of Fiends.
Some voiced firm Will to conquer Heav'n,
Other voices held that idiotic.
At last they decided someone should go
Journey forth unto God's new World,
And bring back Intelligence thereof.
And wily Satan said, "Who among ye dare
To brave th'awful Chaos, the empty gulf
'Twixt Here and Heav'n?"
The multitude of Demons then was silent.
Satan said, "Okay, I'll go," and he did,
And he was like, "Damn, that was easy."
And so he flew from Hell, into Chaos,
On his Way to the strange new World.

Book III

In Heav'nly light sat God upon his Throne,
Watching o'er His creation, and beheld
The flight of th'Enemy expostate.
"Come, mine Son," said God, "Hie thee hither,
And get a load of this."
And Jesus, who was right there anyway,
At the right hand of God, as always,
Looked where the Father was pointing,
Beheld Satan on his cursèd journey.
Said God, "He's going to th'Earth, that Fiend,
To corrupt and pervert the Creatures I hath wrought
In mine own image."
To which replied the Son: "I'll stop him!"
To which the Father: "Nay, son, nay;
Man hath I created Wise and Able,
Well can he withstand Temptation.

And yet, if not, it's not Mine Fault,
For I am without Fault, and Great."
To which replied the son, "You the Man."
To which the Father, "No, You the Man."
At which the cherubs laughed and clapped,
Waved fists and called out, "Woo! Woo! Woo!"
Then God said, "But Man indeed will fall,
To Satan's wily Tricks will he succumb,
Immensely doth this chappeth Mine Hide.
Thus must he lose the Grace in which I clothed him,
And thus must therefore die, and all his children die,
And all their children also, and their children's children,
And so on for ever, all of them. And also their pets."
Harsh words! And the cherubs were sore afraid.
And God said, "Unless one from among ye
Would freely sacrifice yourself for Man,
Would suffer his Punishment for Him,
This sentence I impose, without appeal."
And the heavenly chorus resounded: "As if!"

Up rose the Son, God's only begotten—
An only child, and somewise spoiled—
Solemnly he spoke, quiet was his Voyce,
Yet all Heav'n heard his every word:
He was God's son, they listened pretty good.
"I shall do it, Father. For You, for them.
Freely I offer myself for Man's Salvation."
To which the Father: "But they're idiots!
I didn't mean *you,* I meant one of *them!*"
To which the Son: "But they're cute idiots."
Then said God, "It is done! I accept
Thy errant sacrifice, thy noble error,
And name thee the Incarnation and the Highest,
And now everyone will sing of thy Glory—
Arise, fill Heav'n with Hallelujahs in thy Honor!

And mine too, mine too, for I am God!"
And those cherubs didn't miss a beat.

Meanwhile, Satan had flown for some time,
Time being weird in Chaos, and taking longer
Than it took in other places.
And now had he crossed the long Chaotic void,
and did at last alight on Mount Niphates.

Book IV

Now stood Satan high and in prospect of Eden,
And betook himself to consider his enterprize.
"Now I prepare me to mess with God.
And yet perhaps my vengeance is unjust,
Perhaps I'm overreacting. I fought, I lost,
Is it not too late to say I'm sorry?
Yet alas! If e'er Heav'n took me back
I'd have to sing the praise of God all day,
And sing His virtues and His wisdom,
And that would be an Awfulle Dragge."

Thus resteeling his resolve, Satan leaped
Down unto Earth, and landed in a tree,
The Tree of Life, the Highest Place,
In the form of a Flamingo, and looked
About, surveyed the new Creation.
Then beheld he Adam, and also Eve,
Their naked and wonderful innocence.
He bethought, "What a piece of work is Man!
How noble in reason! How infinite in faculty,
In form and movement how like an angel,
And how much better still is Woman!"
They spoke: he bethought himself to eavesdrop.
"How art thou, dear Eve?" said Adam.

And Eve saieth, "Good, and how art you?"
And Adam saieth, "Good, thanks. Say, Eve,
Hast thou been near the Tree of Knowledge,
That tree whereof if we eat, we're screwed?"
And Eve saieth, "Nay, Adam, I hath not been
Anywhere near the Tree of Knowledge,
That tree of which we were commanded
Not to taste its fruites, lest we die,
Which, not knowing death, doesn't mean much,
But hath scared us pretty good just the same.
Why dost thou ask?"
To which answered Adam, "No reason."
And Satan heard this and bethought himself,
"I've got to see this tree."

Book V

God wanted to make sure Man had no excuse,
Could claim not Ignorance of the Law,
So down from Heaven sent he Raphael,
Down to Paradise, Adam to remind
That Satan was Bad, and God was good,
And eating from the Tree of Knowledge—! Well.
Down he flew, to meet with Adam and Eve.

Those two had their morning psalms and prayer,
Their being-visited-by-an-Angel prayer,
Their grateful-for-their-bower prayer,
And finally they were done with all that.
So Raphael gave Adam his message:
Reminded him of the Goodness of God,
Forewarned him of the Badness of Satan,
And last, in language unambiguous,
Warned lest he eat of the Tree of Knowledge,
Forbidden by God—off limits—don't touch.

Adam listened, nodded, went, "Uh-huh, okay,"
Then asked about the recent Battel
Between God and Satan, high in Heav'n.

Book VI

Raphael told Adam the whole Story:
How for two long days the fight was even.
And on the third day, God was like, "Enough."
Then did Jesus mount His bryght Chariot.
He bade the good Angels stand aside,
Called out, "*Giddyap, giddyap—yeeeeha!*"
Straight rolled Jesus into enemy rankes!
Unstoppable with His thundrous Wrath,
Back He drove the Rebel Rankes—Back! Back!
Until He'd pressed them 'gainst the very walls,
Then knocking them through, so they all fell
Down to that awful fiery prison
That rowling Inferno of liquid Flayme,
That we've already talked so much about.
Then Jesus rode back calmly, coolly:
Rode back to His Father, Triumphant,
Resplendent, Glorious, Victorious,
And a little smug.

Book VII

Then saieth Adam, "Tell me about us,
How came we two to be created?"
And Raphael told how after the fight,
God said, "A New World shall I create,
And fill it will I with brand new creatures
And see if they're a little more grateful."
Jesus and some cherubs built it for him,
in six days only they built Creation.

And then, when done, on the seventh day
Hymns and praises sang they, all of them,
About how good it was to be Good,
And how sad it was that not everyone
Could be as wonderful as they were,
Such as certain Angels, for example,
Whose asses had just been kicked to Hell.
And on and on, hymns and praises, endless.

Book VIII

Then saieth Adam, "Tell me about the sky,
About the planets' movements, and the stars,
The workings of the celestial spheres,
The cloakèd secrets of time, and tides,
And why I'm here right now, and what love is:
What it's all about, Raphy?"
And thus did Raphael answer him: "No."

Once more warned he Adam and Eve:
Once more told how Good Angels were Good,
And Bad Angels were Bad, specially Satan,
Who was actually the Worst, and how
They must not eat from the Tree of Knowledge,
No matter what, for any reason, ever,
Under any conditions, period.
And then he left.

And Adam and Eve said prayers for him,
And sang hymns, and were grateful, and all that,
Because they didn't know any better:
They wouldn't have known a Setup
If it bit them in the Ass.

Book IX

When morning came, Adam and Eve awoke
Gave thanks for the day, sang a hymn of praise,
Said a prayer, fed and walked their bower,
Then set about their labours for the day.
Saieth Eve, "Let us go forth sep'rately,
Saving some time by splitting our workload."
And Adam replied, "Madam, I'm Adam."
Saieth Eve: "That was funny the first hundred times.
Now go: quicker will it be, sep'rately,
And there'll be more time for singing praise
And hymns, and prayers, and being thankful."
Said Adam, "Remember ye our warning!
How the Tempter would come and tempt us?
We're stronger together: we must not split."
Said Eve, "Because you think you're too stupid,
Or because you think you're too weak?"
And so they went off sep'rately.

And so withal came Eve to be alone,
Gath'ring flowers, joy and gladness at heart,
And the sun dappled her rosy young skin,
And dew glittered in her shining hair,
And she was absolutely bare-assed naked,
And utterly unashamed.
And Satan as a Serpent watched her,
Made sure she'd be able to see him.
And she saw him, and noticed his stare,
And went about her business all the same,
Pretending not to have noticed him there,
Only her pride a little gratified
By th'appreciation of the Serpent,
Who was not yet then a snake, but had legs,

And a pleasing form. Then he saw his moment.
He spoke. "Beautiful creature," saieth he,
"Enchanting marvel! Celest'l delight!
Who art thou that thus bedraped in splendor
Move about unaware of thy charms?"
Eve blushed, and smiled, and said "But thou!
Thou serpent, oft have I spied thee before,
Many times, and bethought you without Voice,
Or Reason, or Facultyes sufficient
To appreciate mine womanly form—
Mine graceful curves, mine firm young breasts;
Ne'er yet had thou noticed this perfection."
And the Serpent (it's Satan, remember)
Answered thus: "It is true, Glorious Eve,
That I have of late been without Voice,
Been without Reason, lacked appreciation.
The Fruits of a certain tree I tasted,
Then suddenly could speak, and reason, and
Marvel at thy bodacious ta-tas."
Saieth Eve, "What manner of Fruit was that
That thus improved thy dullèd senses?"
Saieth the Serpent, "Come on, follow me."
And to the Tree of Knowledge led her.
Saieth Eve, "Alas! 'Tis the only tree
Of which we are forbidden to eat."
Then said the Serpent, "That cannot be.
Hath thy Creator not planted it here?
Hath He not given thee appetites?
Is't not marvelous that I, Serpent,
So recently mute, insensible,
Stand thus improved from the taste of one fruit?
'Tis surely no harm I suffered! None! Zero!
And if this fruit can improve me thus,
Imagine what it can do for thee!

Sure thy Creator meant a diff'rent tree—
Perhaps he meant that one over there.
I bet he did."

Eve so marveled at the Serpent's speech,
So wondered at Fruit that could thus transform
Senselessness to sense, she bethought anew.
"Thou art right," she saieth, "fruit shall I eat!
And after all, it's a good-looking fruit,
And Fat free, and few of Caloryes, and
Loaded with Vytamins and Mineralles."
Thus ate she fruit of the Forbidden Tree,
The Tree of Knowledge, of which Raphael
Had told her and Adam, "Don't eat from it!"
And after she had tasted the Fruit,
She felt transformed, all the world seemed diff'rent.
"Stop staring at my chest," she said,
"Mine eyes are up here." The Serpent smiled,
For it was no ordinary Serpent
(As you may recall I had mentioned),
But Satan himself, who now moved away:
His work done, he hightailed it out of there.

And Eve now left alone bethought herself
Some of the Fruit for Adam to bring.
Not far off she found him, and betold him
About the Serpent, how well now he spoke!,
How attunèd to beauty had he become!,
How sensible to womanly charms,
Whom mere dumb Brute had so recently been!
And about the Tree, its transforming Fruit.
Saieth Adam, "Eve! What hast thou done!
Forbidden were we to eat of that Tree,
And have ye not broken that commandment?"
Saieth Eve, "It's only Fruit, no biggie."

Saieth Adam, "Thou hast sealed thy Doom,
Brought the Disfavor of our Creator
Upon thyself, O wretched woman!"
Saieth Eve unto him, "Yes, mine love,
Yes! 'Tis true, I am wretched, I am weak,
And therefore cannot suffer this alone:
If you really loved me you'd eat some too."

Saieth Adam, "For thy sweet love, Eve,
I will taste of the Fruit, and share thy Doom,
Only for Love of thee do I do this,
This unbelievably stupid Thing,
This incredibly dangerous Thing,
This idiotic Thing I would not do
For anything but thy tender Love,
This really dumb Thing—" Saieth Eve, "Just eat."
And Adam ate the Fruit. And Eve said, "Good boy."

The Fruit then eaten, Adam looked at Eve:
With fresh eyes saw her pleasing form,
And saieth unto her, "Nice rack, babe."
She looked her Adam over, saw his state,
And saieth, "Get that thing away from me."
Saieth Adam, "Thou knowest thou wants it."
Eve backed away, covering herself.
"Thou art a pig," cried Eve, "thou'rt disgusting!
Leave me alone, O, leave me alone!"
Adam replied: "Come to Daddy, baby."
And Eve shrieked and ran, and Adam followed.

Book X

Saieth God, "They have done That which I forbade,
And now let Punishment be announced."
He turned to the Son, and said unto him,

"Thou knowest what to do, belovèd Son."
Said Jesus, "I'm on it like white on rice!"
And Jesus descended to the Earth.

Adam and Eve in the Garden he found,
Bickering and calling each other names.
"Be silent," He commanded; they obeyed.
"All Paradise was given thou," He said,
"And all the Pleasures it affordeth.
Thou had all this cool Stuff, it was all Good,
Thou shouldst have been well contented, but *noooo* . . .
Thou just had to go and eat that Fruit,
Even though we toldest thou not to."
Saieth Eve then unto Jesus, "What fruit?"
Saieth Adam, "We didn't eat anything."
Saieth Jesus, "Nay, I hath seen it all,
And my Father who art in Heav'n,
Hallowed be His name, he saw it too.
So shut thy pie-holes and listen up."
And He told them of how they would suffer,
And their Children would suffer, on and on,
He just couldn't seem to tell them enough
About how much they would have to suffer.
Then at last He went away.

Book XI

Later on, way back up there in Heav'n,
The Son approached the Father and said,
"Behold thy creatures, Adam and Eve,
Hear their repentance, their prayers rise up.
They feel awful, they're really sorry.
Can't we cut them just a little slack?"
And God was like, "All right, all right, all right.
Michael! Come ye hither. Get some cherubs.

Hie thee unto Adam and Eve. Tell them:
My belovèd Son hath interceded,
And Mercy divine hath blessed them both—
But I want them out of that damn garden!"
So Michael and his Cherubs went down,
Found Adam and Eve, still praying,
Weeping, begging forgiveness, repentant.
Saieth Michael, "All right, you guys, enough:
You can knock off the waterworks.
You caught a break, Mercy divine is yours—
But you've got to get out of here."
And wretched Eve began to weep anew,
She loved Paradise, could not bear to leave.
Saieth Michael, "Oh, man. Come on, Adam,
Let us away to somewhere we can talk."
To the top of a hill he led him,
And said, "I'm gonna 'splain you some things."
But first it was time for another book.

Book XII

Thus Michael 'splained things to Adam:
"Outside Paradise, it's all a big mess.
Thy children, and Eve's, will suffer yet,
Though not as bad as we thought at first,
Because the Son said he would take the hit.
But that's much later. First, bad news:
One of your sons kills the other,
Thereby shall Murder enter the world;
Hate and crime shall there be aplenty;
And fear and cruelty, and violence
Begetting violence. And God will
See all this and purge the world with a Flood.
Of course that won't really change much.
Down the Son will then come as promised,

The fall at last to take for you guys.
And even after him there'll be Murder
And Violence and Suffering, and Starvation
In the land of Plenty, and Cruelty under the
Life-giving Sun, and Wars in the name of God,
And Wars in the name of State, and Wars in the
Name of Stable Petroleum Prices.
Death, Disease, Anguish will there be always,
But there will at least be knowledge
That the Son of God hath died for your sins."
Saieth Adam, "Thanks. That's reassuring.
I am comforted now."

Michael didn't understand Sarcasm,
So he smiled and they went to get Eve.
Adam said, "Come on, babe, we're outta here.
We never liked this stupid place anyway."
Eve nodded and smiled and took his hand.
They followed Michael out of Paradise
And he locked the Gates behind them
And appointed guards to watch over it.
(But not the same guards that let Satan in:
Better cherubs these, way harder to trick.)
Then Adam and Eve turned back and looked,
Looked one long last teary-eyed time,
At the Paradise they'd lost for ever.

"It's all your stupid fault," saieth Adam.
Replieth Eve: "Shut up."

—The End—

Sense and Sensibility

by Jane Austen

(1811)

"A woman of seven-and-twenty," said Marianne, after pausing a moment, "can never hope to feel or inspire affection again."

The French and American revolutions at the end of the eighteenth century announced the dawn of a new age. It was an age of reason, wherein governments would rule by the consent of the governed, every citizen would be accorded certain inalienable rights, and aristocrats would have their heads chopped off. This was a radical shift in political philosophy, which had for centuries operated on the golden rule: whoever had the gold made the rules.[1]

Despite the liberal tendencies of the age, women were still discouraged from writing books; novels were still being written in the formal style, and it was feared that women would corrupt that classic form with their penchant for multiple climaxes. British writer Jane Austen was therefore compelled to write screenplays, and subsequently languished in obscurity until the invention of cinematography. Even then it was still many decades before producers finally recognized her talent and flooded the market with films of her work.

While Austen's majestic use of language is surely diminished in its translation to English, it is hoped that the following translation conveys at least a sense of her exquisite command of her native tongue.

The Dashwood family had been in Sussex for as long as anyone in those parts could remember, which, given the life expectancy of the period, was not too terribly long. They owned a vast amount of property, and were forever tiptoeing out into the night and moving the boundary markers to make it even larger. They themselves dwelt in the very heart of their humongous real estate holdings—if the heart is to be held as dwelling in the center of the body, rather than a little above and to the left of it—on an estate called Norland Park.

---

[1] The Wizard of Id, *Remember the Golden Rule, op. cit.*

The late owner of the estate had never married or had children because, sadly, he had lost his testicles. Fortunately his sister had been an ugly, stupid woman and had therefore never married, and she took care of him until she died. After her death the gentleman's nephew, Henry Dashwood, the son of the gentleman's only sibling clever enough to have reproduced, moved in to care for him. Henry brought his wife and three daughters to Norland Park, and the dying old gentleman was quite fond of them all—too fond, perhaps, of the daughters, whom he loved to bounce on his knee until they were well into their teens. Indeed: *especially* when they were well into their teens. The old man was so terribly fond of them that it had long been his hope to bequeath to them in his will all the family property, including Norland Park, the servants, the silver, the china, the porcelain, the horses, and his extensive collection of imported lawn gnomes.

However, the mother of these girls was not Henry Dashwood's first wife. The original Mrs. Dashwood had died long ago and left him a son (although not in that order). This son was now a grown man by the name of John Dashwood. He was a twit, and had therefore married a woman named Fanny.

These two had, by some grotesque biology, produced a son, and the entry into this world of a male Dashwood with two working testicles had sealed the doom of the Misses Dashwood. Both Henry and his dying uncle were now compelled by the dictates of primogeniture to redirect the entire inheritance to the littlest Mr. Dashwood, John and Fanny's son.

At last the old Mr. Dashwood died and was laid to rest with his testicles, which he had kept in a glass jar on his nightstand all these many years. A year or so later, Henry lay on his own deathbed—despite the fact that his uncle's was still in perfectly good condition—and he called John to his side.

"The law of primogeniture," Henry wheezed, "requires that I bequeath to you all that my uncle left for me to hold in your name, and your son's, until the time of my own death, which now appears imminent."

"I love primogeniture," said John.

"I cannot bequeath more than a pittance for my wife or your half-sisters," Henry gurgled.

"One pittance should suffice," his nephew replied, pinching a bit of snuff from his snuffbox. "One mustn't spoil women with pittances."

"It is my utmost wish," Henry continued with difficulty, "that you make use of these vast resources, complete possession of which has fallen upon you without your having done a great deal to deserve it, to ensure that your stepmother and stepsisters, whose own expected fortunes have been so capriciously denied them, due to no fault of their own, are taken care of, and that ERK—" And here Henry died, his death no doubt having been accelerated by complications of syntax and grammar.

John Dashwood fully intended to honor his father's dying wish, and he told his wife of his intention to give his stepmother and half-sisters ten thousand pounds each.

"You cruel man!" she exclaimed. "Have you come so far in life with so little idea of the snares that are set for wealthy women by unscrupulous gentlemen? Can you be so thick-headed as to doubt for a minute that such aggrandizement of your sisters' fortune would surely guarantee their doom? I hope I have not married such a hardhearted man as would wish such misery upon his half sisters!"

"Heavens, no!" John replied.

"Very well, then you have had your jest with me. How better can you take care of your sisters than by preserving their innocent souls from the cares and worries attendant with financial complication? When the gentlemen come calling your sisters will know they are coming not with some design on their fortune, but from genuine craven desire."

"Very true," John agreed, "but what about my stepmother? Surely her situation with regard to marriage differs?"

Fanny shrugged. "Stepmothers turn into bats at night and fly about sucking people's blood. You must steal in upon her while she sleeps one morning and drive a stake through her heart, then dismember her and bury her bones in the shade of a yumyum tree."

"Heavens! I'll do no such thing!"

"Well, then, the least you can do is keep her from getting any money. Lord alone knows what such a monster would do with it!"

The issue was settled. John, Fanny, and their son moved into Norland Park at once, and Mrs. Dashwood and the three Misses Dashwood were asked to kindly get their affairs in order and retire to some place that was not Norland Park—for example, Mexico or Japan.

It was a difficult time for the Dashwood women. Lacking money and the means to make it, and without any relations thoughtful enough to die and leave them some, they were now unattractive marriage prospects for the well-to-do men and boys who might otherwise have been interested. The best they could do was try to find somewhere to live on their meager budget; somewhere they could live in modest comfort and pass the time sewing, and playing the pianoforte, and criticizing each other's décolletage until they had the good sense to die. They found such a place.

Now perhaps we should acquaint ourselves a little better with these poor creatures. Mrs. Dashwood was a lovely lady who was bringing up three very lovely girls; all of them had hair of gold, like their mother, the youngest one in curls. Elinor, the eldest—and, by happy coincidence, the oldest—was a sensible nineteen-year-old. The middle daughter, Marianne, was seventeen and had her mother's impetuous nature; she had also been endowed by nature with a magnificent bosom that seemed always to be glistening with dew and heaving with youthful ardor. Lastly there was the youngest, Margaret, a rowdy twelve-year-old without the slightest idea what was going on, whose silly childhood antics were a great source of relief to her wretched sisters and mother, who might have slit their own miserable throats if Margaret hadn't made them giggle so.

But not all had been so bleak in the weeks before the put-upon Dashwood women were exiled from Norland Park: Fanny's brother, Mr. Edward Ferrars, had dropped by on one of the pointless meandering journeys of the idle rich. Elinor's interest in him appeared to be reciprocated. Mr. Ferrars was of a shy and quiet disposition; he was so abundantly bestowed with all the various virtues that one could barely stand him, and his speech was so polite and deferential as to make no sense whatsoever. He was the very sort of milksop to appeal to Elinor, who graciously forgave his being the likely heir to a vast fortune.

Elinor's mother and sisters were confident that Mr. Ferrars would sooner or later propose marriage, but he expressed no views on the subject despite the fact that his warm regard for Elinor was easily discerned: he had been so forward once as to have let the back of his hand brush against her elbow. At last the four Dashwood women quit Norland Park to inhabit a cottage in Devonshire, practically on the other side of England. Mr. Ferrars said good-bye to Elinor without even hinting at the possibility of some future prospect of matrimony.

Their new home was called Barton Cottage, and it was owned by and on the property of one Sir John Middleton, a handsome and jovial forty-year-old with a handsome and jovial fortune. His wife, Lady Middleton, was a pretty but fragile woman of six or seven and twenty. She had, to Sir John's horror, produced fourteen and a half children, the oldest being six and the eldest being eight. Lady Middleton's mother, Mrs. Jennings, was a plump widow who was fond of telling dirty jokes. She was sometimes quite humorous, and although it was often in a very naughty sort of way it could not be disputed that her heart was in the right place (i.e., above and a little to the left of center). Unfortunately, she was disposed to employ her little jests and provocative humour always at the worst possible times. To speak plainly, she was a big fat loudmouth and it was a constant struggle for everyone to refrain from whacking her. Then there was Colonel Brandon, an old friend of Sir John's. He was a very serious, very dry thirty-five-year-old gentleman who fell in love with Marianne the moment he laid eyes on her. It was whispered among the servants at Barton Park that Colonel Brandon had once killed a man. In fact he had killed several men, but it was not yet a prosecutable crime in Britain to bore a man to death. This was the jolly crew whose particular pleasure it was to grind the Misses Dashwood into wretched, soulless, idle creatures like themselves.

One day Marianne took Margaret out for a long walk. It began raining while they were still far from the house, and they decided to run home because they were such impetuous little sweethearts. Marianne tripped and tumbled down a steep hill, twisting her pretty little ankle in the process. Luckily for her, and for those of us following her story, a handsome young man of dashing manner and in dashing clothes chose precisely that moment to ride up on his black steed.

He dismounted and ran to her side, heedless of anything but her welfare. He scooped her up and carried her home. She had never before been touched by a man, and though she was enthralled by his person she could not overcome her fear of being put with child.

This dashing figure, as it turned out, was a certain Mr. Willoughby. He was living with an old dowager aunt at nearby Allenham Court, and all her property and money and servants were to pass into his possession at the time of her death, which, to his great dissatisfaction, she continued to postpone. He became a frequent visitor at Barton Cottage, and he and Marianne found no sweeter delight than the continuous tormenting of Colonel Brandon: how they loved to tease him! They made fun of his clothes, they mocked his conversation, and Willoughby was always giving him wedgies. It was all great fun.

Elinor was not pleased by her sister's passion. In a private moment she told her so. "Be careful," she said.

"Careful? Only you would be careful in love, Elinor, you who blushed with shame whenever Mr. Ferrars happened to have inadvertently breathed air that could conceivably have been expelled from your own lungs."

"That is quite enough!" Elinor exclaimed, blushing. "In our precarious situation, one cannot be too careful. Yes, Mr. Ferrars may have breathed air that had . . . that I had previously . . . yes, you know everything, I do not deny it! And once we very nearly made eye contact. But I never lost my sense or my dignity."

"I love Willoughby, and he loves me," Marianne said. "That is all *I* require of a man's character."

"Tell me at least," Elinor said, struggling to contain herself, "that you have examined his dental records and had his handwriting analyzed. No? Oh, Marianne . . . You will regret it!"

The argument ended there. A few days later Mrs. Dashwood and her daughters received an invitation from Sir John and Lady Middleton to join them at Barton Park for an evening of entertainment. Marianne invited Willoughby, of course—the impetuous thing!—and the fivesome reached Barton Park that Saturday afternoon in exuberant spirits.

Colonel Brandon arrived a few moments after the Dashwoods and Willoughby, and Sir John and Lady Middleton came out to greet them, along with Mrs. Jennings. As the formal greetings were being exchanged, a messenger came running out of breath from the post road.

"Urgent and mysterious confidential note for Colonel Brandon," he gasped.

While Colonel Brandon read the note the messenger keeled over dead of exhaustion. Sir John sent for servants to haul away his carcass. Colonel Brandon kept reading. The servants came and went. The assembled guests sighed and glanced at their pocket watches and rolled their eyes. The sun began to dip below the horizon. Colonel Brandon was a slow reader.

"I regret that I must away to London immediately," the Colonel finally said in his usual lugubrious tone, putting Mrs. Jennings and Lady Middleton to sleep.

"Oh, colonel!" cried Mrs. Dashwood. "You mustn't! Pattycakes just isn't the same without you!"

"I'm quite afraid that this matter is of the utmost urgency," he replied. Now Margaret nodded off, and several of the horses lowered their eyelids. "You may trust that I would not rush off so hastily unless it were a matter of gravest consequence," he added, and now Elinor drifted off, along with her mother and Sir John.

"Don't let the door hit your arse on the way out," Willoughby said, and he and Marianne laughed gleefully as the somber Colonel Brandon mounted his horse.

"I'm afraid I don't understand," the Colonel said. "We're already outside. There's no door to pass through. I judge by your hilarity that this misplaced expression of concern possesses some irony or humourous hidden meaning, but I'm afraid it escapes me at the moment." And without even noticing that Willoughby and Marianne had fallen asleep, Colonel Brandon spurred his steed and awayed to London.

A week later the Dashwoods were invited to another shindig at Barton Park. Marianne begged to be left home alone. Her sisters and mother were baffled by this impetuous girl's inexplicable desire to be left behind whilst they were all playing Ring Around the Rosy and Rock, Paper, Scissors with the revelers at Barton Park. Elinor began to apprehend Marianne's purposes when, checking in on her to say good-bye just before they set out, she found her sister removing her gloves before the mirror.

"I love and trust you deeply, Marianne," Elinor said, "so I will not inquire why you intend to lounge about the house alone without gloves. I am confident you would not betray our trust and endanger your own future by allowing Willoughby sight of your delicate, naked wrists. . . . I am confident you deserve our trust."

As Elinor, Margaret, and Mrs. Dashwood returned that evening, they encountered a flustered Willoughby on his way out.

"I am quite sorry," he said. "It is my deepest regret that . . . But no! I will not torture myself!" And he ran out.

Elinor discovered Marianne in her bedroom, weeping inconsolably. Her gloves were on, but they were rumpled.

"Oh, Marianne!" she cried. "Have you not deserved my trust?"

Marianne struggled to contain her impetuous emotions. "We engaged in no improper relations," she said. "But he must away and would give me no account of whither or wherefore!"

"No account at all?"

"None!"

"Oh, dear Marianne! They are adverbs. He might have told you at least as much."

Marianne's sorrow overcame her, and she wept again.

For forty days and forty nights she wept. The cottage was inundated with the deluge of her tears. The cats drowned, along with the servants who couldn't swim. This caused the Misses Dashwood even deeper grief, as good cats were hard to find.

Elinor, Margaret, and Mrs. Dashwood took advantage of every invitation offered by Sir John and Lady Middleton to remove themselves from the flooded cottage. Elinor, it may be admitted, also sought to escape because she was beginning to despair of ever seeing Mr. Edward Ferrars again; she had heard little of or from him since leaving Norland Park, and what news she had from Fanny and John tended more toward the doings of Mr. *Robert* Ferrars, Edward's foppish brother, whose drooling obsequiousness and nervous giggle had greatly endeared him to her brother, John. It was during this series of frequent visits that Elinor, Margaret, and their mother were introduced first to a Mr. and Mrs. Palmer, who didn't really matter, and then to some of Lady Middleton's cousins, the Misses Steele: Lucy and Anne.

Miss Anne Steele was a silly young woman whose only ambition was to marry a doctor and bear children, preferably his. Miss Lucy Steele was not much more ambitious, but her ambition was of more consequence to Elinor: for, as she confided to Elinor during a private moment at Barton Park while the others were embroiled in a game of Peekaboo, she had secretly been engaged to Mr. Edward Ferrars for some five years. Indeed, not just any five years, but those just passed.

Elinor suddenly understood Mr. Ferrars's recalcitrance. She understood why he could not in good faith have spoken to her about matrimony. And, just as suddenly, she realized how readily her problems could be solved: she picked up a knitting needle from the table beside her and jammed it up Miss Steele's nose with such force that the young woman was almost certainly dead well before the end of the needle protruded out the back of her skull.

No one had been especially fond of Miss Steele, so Elinor's explanation that the needle had simply slipped out of her hand was accepted by one and all with happy credulity.

At Lucy's wake Mr. Edward Ferrars confessed to Elinor that he had contracted a secret engagement with the late Miss Steele while he was still a young man and unable to restrain the natural impulse to glance furtively at persons of the opposite sex, and to daydream about touching their accessories. He had considered it a point of honor to see the engagement through, but now that Lucy was dead he was again a free man, and he proposed. Elinor quite readily accepted.

Colonel Brandon had returned from his journey. He tried to tell anyone who would listen where he had been and why he had gone, but his explanations had their usual numbing effect and no one ever remained awake long enough to hear him out. People remembered only snippets, and all that was known for sure was that Willoughby was a wicked man after all, a scullery maid had borne a child, a shot had rung out, a dog had barked, a baroness had died, and the colonel, dull as he may have been, was not at all bad. Also there was something about pirates and buried treasure, but no one could make sense of it.

Despite all these happy goings-on, Marianne had at last become quite sick from all her crying. She became feverish and very nearly died. At the height of her delirium, she fell in love with the Colonel, and they were married soon thereafter. As she never fully recovered, she was quite happy with him for the rest of her life.

—The End—

Notes on the film: *Like so many other of the world's finest writers, Austen was not honored posthumously until after she died.* Sense and Sensibility *won the Academy Award for Best Screenplay in 1995, but not without controversy. Literary critics decried its convoluted and misogynistic departures from Austen's original script, outraged, for example, that the character of Elinor had been transformed from*

Austen's strong, no-nonsense young woman into a hamstrung little ninny without the courage to stick her tongue out at Lucy Steele, much less shove a knitting needle through her head. On the other hand, the movie had a lot of pretty costumes and scenery, and Kate Winslet's chest heaved pleasantly in the role of Marianne's bosom.

A Christmas Carol

by Charles Dickens

(1843)

"This is the even-handed dealing of the world!" he said. "There is nothing on which it is so hard as poverty; and there is nothing it professes to condemn with such severity as the pursuit of wealth!"

In the middle of the nineteenth century, London saw the climax of the Industrial Revolution. This was Western Civilization's first big step toward television and diet cola and was therefore good. Unfortunately, it required a lot of smokestacks and sweatshops and was therefore also bad.

Charles Dickens was born in 1812. His father was imprisoned for debt when Charles was only twelve, and Charles was sent to work in a warehouse. It was there that the little Dickens developed his hypothesis that child labor was a bad thing. With no formal training, he went on to become a journalist, which allowed him to identify even more bad things about the Industrial Revolution. He was so angry he began writing humorous newspaper sketches, and these established his popularity. Eventually he began writing novels, many of which dealt with all the bad things he had identified, such as soot. He wrote a godawful lot of them. Finally he died.

It was the best of *The Times,* it was the worst of *The Times;* it was the special year-end edition and it contained no mention of Marley's death, for he had been as dead as a doornail for many years.

Mind! I don't mean to say that I know, of my own knowledge, what there is particularly dead about a doornail. My family name being Pirrip, and my Christian name being Philip, my infant tongue could make of both names nothing longer or more explicit than Pip, and so I called myself Pip, and everyone else called me Pip, except for one gentleman who insisted on calling me Chuckles. So you will understand my regrettable ignorance regarding the deadness of doornails.

But certainly, Marley was dead as one.

• • •

Ebenezer Scrooge, however, was not dead. Quite the contrary, and to everyone's irritation, he remained very much alive and carried on the business of Scrooge and Marley alone. Scrooge was a coldhearted, tightfisted, miserly old fellow, whose principal pleasure it was to drive trusting and kindhearted people into financial ruin. (When this was not possible he was amenable to striking them with blunt instruments.) He didn't greet people on the street, attended no social gatherings, belonged to no fraternal organizations, never exercised, didn't floss, and he refused to set out leftovers for the puppies that came whimpering to his door now and again seeking solace from the bleak and bitter London winters.

What were puppies to him? Stinking little vermin-ridden bundles of filth, who consumed an inordinate amount of resources in order to produce only two commodities, both of which were manufactured in superfluous quantities despite their negligible value—to say nothing of their odour. Puppies were an economic dead end.

He was fond of saying so.

One Christmas Eve old Scrooge sat busy in his counting-house, admiring each shiny coin as he took it from the great glowing pile before him and dropped it into the pretty pink piggy bank beside him. (Let it not be said that Scrooge did not love, for I do not know what else to call the sentiment he attached to that pig. He called her Miss Ogilvy, and often stroked her ceramic snout with gentle affection.) Through his office door he could see his clerk entering upon the third stage of hypothermia. The clerk cast an imploring look at Scrooge.

"What's that?" cried Scrooge.

"Beg pardon?" said the clerk.

"That imploring look—what was that?"

"Not imploring," the clerk said, "never imploring, sir."

"Very well then." Scrooge turned back to his counting.

"Yes, sir!" cried the clerk. "Yes, it was imploring, I confess. If you please, sir—it's chafing again!"

Scrooge did not even look up from his counting. "There are men enough in London," said he, "who would be happy to work on a shorter leash than that."

"It isn't the length, sir, I don't object to the length, it's a very liberal leash, sir, as you say, sir—only it chafes something terrible about the neck, sir. . . ."

At that moment the door to Scrooge's shop swung open, and a handsome young gentleman stepped in. His face was flushed with holiday spirits, and he emanated goodwill.

"Merry Christmas, Uncle!" he cried.

"Off with his head!" roared Scrooge.

The clerk only whimpered. Scrooge rose from his desk and began rummaging for a blunt instrument.

The handsome young gentleman smiled at Scrooge indulgently, for he was full of love, forgiveness, and trust, having been raised by Scrooge's loving, forgiving, and trusting sister, Fanny, who had been so very good and kind that angels had come down from heaven and kidnapped her many years ago. He therefore took no notice of Scrooge's apparently violent intentions, for he knew them to be merely another symptom of his uncle's annual Yuletide paroxysm. Besides, he was not only younger and handsomer than his uncle, he was faster.

"Uncle," he said, "I've only come by as I do every Christmas Eve, to beg you—for my dear departed mother's sake—to beg that you might join my family for Christmas dinner to-morrow."

Scrooge only muttered, weighing a bottle of ink in one hand and calculating the probable effect of its impact on his nephew's skull.

"Very well, then," said the nephew, turning to depart.

"Merry Christmas, Fred!" the clerk declared in a spasm of holiday cheer.

"And a merry Christmas to you, Bob Crotchitch," Fred replied, and he was out the door before Scrooge could take proper aim.

Thus stymied by his nephew, Scrooge hurled the bottle at the clerk. It made a pleasing sound as it struck his head, and Scrooge looked on with satisfaction as Bob Crotchitch slumped to the floor.

Not long afterward, two portly gentlemen entered the offices. They, too, were flush-faced and jolly, for they were good-hearted men with unblemished souls, unlike a certain someone with whom you are already familiar. These portly and good-hearted gentleman were raising Christmas charity funds, and as they were more good-hearted than bright, they had come to solicit donations from the profitable firm of Scrooge and Marley.

"At this festive season of the year," said one of them, "it is more than usually desirable that we should make some provision for the poor and destitute. Many thousands are in want of common necessities; hundreds of thousands are in want of common comforts."

"Are there no prisons?" Scrooge asked.

"Plenty of prisons," the sympathetic gentleman replied. His companion nodded.

"And the Union Workhouses?" demanded Scrooge.

"They are still in operation," the compassionate gentleman answered, "though I wish I could say they were not."

"And the red hot pokers?"

"Beg pardon?" said the gracious gentleman.

"Run," said his companion.

"Aha!" cried Scrooge, brandishing the poker from his furnace. He chased the gentlemen from his offices and halfway up the street, catching each of them once or twice in the back. When he returned to his office the clerk was picking himself up wearily from the floor, groaning pitiably and clutching his head with one hand.

"I suppose you'll be wanting tomorrow off?" Scrooge asked.

The clerk nodded timidly, and Scrooge struck him emphatically with the poker.

Much later that evening Scrooge sat in a chair by the fireplace in his bedroom, supping at his gruel with Miss Ogilvy, when suddenly the fire roared up and his bed curtains fluttered violently. There came a pounding from the lower floor, the sound of doors and shutters slamming open and shut, and then of heavy footsteps climbing the stairs. He heard the steps continue along the hallway, toward his room. And then, passing directly through the door as though it were no more substantial than a breath of wind, into the room there came a dread and ghostly figure. He was bound head to foot in such a tangle of irons and chains that it seemed impossible he should have made it up to Scrooge's room without having tripped and broken his neck on the stairs.

The ghost raised his arms and groaned horribly. "Ebenezer!" he moaned woefully, "Ebenezer Scrooge! These chains that I wear in death, I forged in life!"

Scrooge admired the gentleman's craftsmanship. The chains were solid and well-wrought.

"They're good chains," he said.

"Ebenezer!" groaned the ghost.

Scrooge cowered.

"Ebenezer!"

"Yes . . . ?" Scrooge answered meekly.

"*Ebenezer!*" howled the ghost.

"What?" Scrooge asked.

"I just like saying 'Ebenezer,' " said the ghost, and he sat down beside the fire.

• • •

It turned out that the ghost was none other than Jacob Marley, dead Marley, Scrooge's old partner. Marley explained that because he had failed in life to do any good by his fellow man, and had indeed done nothing more generous for the human race than to leave it, he was cursed forever to roam the earth and drag his chains, etc., and that Scrooge, being a bastard of a similar stripe, was destined to a similar fate. Scrooge objected to this suggestion, and said as much.

"Would you avoid this dread sentence?" asked Marley, as though incredulous that Scrooge could find anything preferable.

"Yes, Jacob."

"There is one hope for you, one chance, and it is in my power to give it you."

"Tell me, Jacob! Whatever it may be, tell me!"

"Three spirits will visit you," the ghost began.

"Never mind," Scrooge said.

The ghost shook and wailed. "Then you will be cursed like me!"

Scrooge pursed his lips, and stroked Miss Ogilvy nervously. "Very well. Three ghosts. What then?"

"You shall meet the spirits of Christmas Past, Present, and Future. And then we shall see," the ghost said, rising. "And then we shall see...."

And with that he floated toward the window, cast one last despairing look back at Scrooge, and drifted out into the night.

Scrooge rushed to the window and gazed out after him. The street was full of souls, all of them in chains, many of them persons of his acquaintance.

"Fancy that," said Scrooge. "I wonder who does their banking?"

He closed the window and went to bed.

He woke up sometime later. His bed curtains were being drawn open by a ghostly hand. The ghostly hand was connected to a ghostly wrist, which was affixed to a ghostly arm, and so on and so forth, none of it surprising insofar as Scrooge was being visited by a ghost. And no ordinary ghost, but a ghost above whom glowed an otherworldly flame, a searing jet of white-hot light.

Scrooge cried out: "Your head is on fire!"

"That flame you see is the light of human charity," the spirit answered. The voice was soft, sweet, and calm.

"A pretty enough distinction," Scrooge grumbled. "I can assure you that such allegorical niceties would be of little comfort to me, if my own skull were to burst into flames. But I see you are a spirit, and perhaps accustomed to such things. Are you, then, one of the spirits whose coming was foretold to me?"

"I am."

"And who are you?"

"That's for me to know," the spirit began, "and for you to find out. Come, take my hand!"

Scrooge held forth a trembling hand. The spirit smiled, and took it in his own.

Suddenly they were standing beside a long and wretched-looking queue of men and women in leg irons, guarded by soldiers on either side. A soldier took the first man in the queue, led him up a flight of steps onto a wooden platform, and laid his head down on a block above which hung a mighty blade.

"It is a far, far better thing that I do, than I have ever done," the man said. "It is a far, far better rest that I go to, than—"

Alas, this interesting monologue was interrupted by the swift and sudden drop of the blade, after which the gentleman did not look likely to resume his reflections. An old woman sitting nearby nodded and cackled hideously, without looking up from her knitting.

"Oops," said the spirit, and in an instant Scrooge was back

in his bed. The world was dark and quiet. Perhaps it had been a dream. He lay back down to sleep.

He awoke sometime later to find rich, bright light flooding through the gaps between his bed curtains. He pulled them open to find his entire room transformed. It was laid out like a king's feast, the floor piled high with turkeys, geese, game, suckling pigs, succulent partridges, glistening trout, caviar, fresh poultice, sautéed *chevaliers,* delicate *faux pas,* sweetmeats, oranges, luscious pears, seething bowls of punch, and above it all there presided a merry giant, a great, broad man in a rich green robe with white trim. He held a torch aloft, and beamed down at Scrooge.

"Are you . . . are you the spirit of Christmas Present?" Scrooge asked nervously.

"I sure as hell ain't the Easter bunny!" roared the giant.

"Well, sir," Scrooge said, "I'm grateful for your visit, sir, insofar as my old partner Marley, or rather his ghost, has given me to understand that these visits—yours and your fellow spirits, I mean, sir—that all of this would somehow redound to my benefit—I mean my salvation, sir, as I have been given to understand: my rescue from sharing his fate, which, if you won't be offended, sir, was not represented to me in a positive light, what with the chains and groans and whatnot, but—"

"Get on with it!" bellowed the spirit.

"Yes, yes, yes," chattered Scrooge. "Yes, as I was saying, sir, good spirit, I don't like to make trouble, sir, but the little fellow last night may have gotten things a bit cockeyed, for I can't make head nor tail out of what he showed me, and after he showed me he only said 'oops' and then disappeared—and as I was saying, sir, and I repeat that I don't like to make trouble for anyone, and I really am extremely grateful for the trouble you and your spirit friend have gone to on my account . . ."

"Hush," said the giant, "touch my robe!"

"Yes," Scrooge said, "of course, only I felt I should tell someone, and I didn't know if there was a proper authority to contact, or—"

"Come," the giant said, and there was a bright flash of light.

At once they stood in a vast, dank room full of young boys, all unwashed and wretchedly dressed. They were seated on benches at a series of long tables running parallel from one end of this great stone hall to the other, eating morosely from small wooden bowls.

Suddenly one young boy rose from his bench and walked toward a big fat fellow who stood at the head of the room, guarding what appeared to be a cauldron. This gentleman (I use the term liberally) stared down at the boy contemptuously as he approached, and only arched his eyebrows as the boy raised his empty bowl up before him.

"Please sir," the boy said tentatively, "I'd like some more." There were murmurs throughout the hall. Furtive heads rose from their bowls and glanced up at the scene taking place.

"Certainly," the man said, "have all you like." And he ladled the boy several ladles full of slop.

"Thank you, sir," said the boy.

"My pleasure," said the man.

"Oops," said the spirit, and once again Scrooge was back in bed.

At length he fell asleep again, and the next time he awoke he found his bed curtains already open. There before him stood a curly-haired young man in topcoat and tails with a sequined vest.

"Are you the spirit of Christmas Future?" Scrooge asked.

"I'm going to make the Statue of Liberty disappear!" the spirit exclaimed.

"I've already seen the spirits of Christmas Past and Present," Scrooge said. "Didn't they tell you? Something's gone wrong—"

"Never before in the annals of magic has such a feat been undertaken!"

"Please," Scrooge said, "I'm certain we can have this all straightened out if only we can make the appropriate persons aware of the confusing state of affairs, but if you're unwilling to discuss it, I'd appreciate if you could just ask me to take your hand, take me somewhere strange, show me something peculiar, say 'oops,' then get me back in bed and have done with it. I'd be very much indebted to you, sir."

"But I'm going to mystify you with the power of magic!" exclaimed the spirit. "I'm the greatest magician the world has ever known!"

"I hardly see the relevance," Scrooge said, and he went back to sleep.

He woke up yet one more time to find a spectral visitor in his bedroom. It was a dark and forbidding creature that stood there, draped in a black cloak that swallowed him up in shadow and concealed his every feature.

"Are *you* the spirit of Christmas Future?" Scrooge asked.

The hooded head nodded.

"You realize that it's been one mistake after another so far?"

The hooded head nodded.

"I suppose we've got to go through with it anyway?"

The hooded head nodded.

"Not very organized up there, are you?"

The hooded head shook from side to side.

Scrooge held out his hand. "Let's get this over with," he said.

Suddenly they were standing in a large and musty room with all its windows sealed. A few tallow candles flickered uncertainly, illuminating the faded and cobwebbed furniture of the room and its only occupant: a ghastly old woman in a dreary yellow dress. On closer examination it appeared to be an old wedding dress, faded and jaundiced by the years.

"Come in," the woman called out in a brittle voice. The door at one end of the room swung open, and a handsome and well-dressed young gentleman entered.

"Good afternoon, Miss Havisham," the young man said sternly.

"Good afternoon, Pip," the lady said.

"You have misled me," the young man said. "You have let me believe it was you who were my secret benefactor. You have taken advantage of my credulity."

"The dickens with your credulity!" she exclaimed. "Don't you want to see Estella? She's back from Europe, and more beautiful than ever."

The young man glowered, but he nodded.

"Call her," Miss Havisham said, clutching the arms of her chair and leaning forward. "Call her!"

The young man went back to the door.

"Estella!" he shouted up the hall, "Estella! Estella!"

A lovely young woman in fancy dress appeared at the end of the hall and moved gracefully toward him.

"Estella," sighed the young man.

"Pip," said the young lady.

"Love her," rasped Miss Havisham, "love her!"

The cloaked spirit shook his head, and there was a blinding flash of light.

Scrooge was alone in his bedroom.

No more spirits troubled him that night. They couldn't have even if they had wanted to: there was no night left. The first gray light of the breaking day streamed into the room. Scrooge hurried to the window and threw it open; a rush of cold air swept over him. It felt marvelous! Rejuvenating! He beheld a young boy pulling a sled along the street beneath the window.

"Boy," Scrooge called out, "boy!"

The boy stopped pulling his sled—with some relief, as there was no snow upon the ground—and looked up at him suspiciously.

"What day is it?" he called down.

"Why, it's Christmas Day, sir!"

"Christmas Day!" Scrooge cried. "It's true, it's Christmas Day! The spirits did it all in one night! I haven't lost a single day! Do you hear, Miss Ogilvy? The office can open at its usual hour!" He rushed to his desk, seized a thick bronze paperweight, and returned to the window. "Stand still, boy!" he cried, and he hurled the paperweight straight at him.

The spirits returned the following Christmas Eve. Having had ample opportunity to practice, they performed their ghostly duties without misadventure. As a result of their intervention, Scrooge reformed his wicked ways and became good and kindhearted, and a boon to whimpering little puppies everywhere.

But that's a story for another day.

—The End—

Moby-Dick

by Herman Melville

(1851)

Swerve me? The path to my fixed purpose is laid with iron rails, whereon my soul is grooved to run. Over unsounded gorges, through the rifled hearts of mountains, under torrents' beds, unerringly I rush! Naught's an obstacle, naught's an angle to the iron way!

Throughout the first half of the nineteenth century, America was struggling to define herself as an independent nation. It therefore became necessary to invent American Literature. Upon publication of James Fenimore Cooper's novels, however, it was determined that American Literature should feature more sailing ships. This caused Herman Melville.

Herman Melville was born in New York City in 1819, and died in New York in 1891. In between, he had a lot of unpleasant little jobs that didn't pay very well. He had sailed around in his youth as a merchant seaman, so he wrote several books about his adventures, many of which featured exotic topless natives. These books did tolerably well, but he still couldn't afford to quit his day job. Finally he wrote Moby-Dick *when he was in his early thirties, and although it didn't generate enough income for Melville to quit working, it did result in the popular stereotype of the peglegged sea captain.*

Scholars have devoted cumulative centuries to the study of the symbols in Melville's masterwork, fixating on the spiritual and existential themes suggested by the malignant white whale of the title, the gold doubloon, Ahab's missing limb, and Queequeg's tattoos, but few scholars have taken time to reflect upon the significance of a book called Moby-Dick *being filled with seamen and spermaceti.*

Call me Ishmael. Some years ago—never mind how long precisely—having little or no money in my purse, and nothing particular to interest me on shore, I thought I would sail about a little and see the watery part of the world. It is my way: whenever I am feeling inclined to step into the street and methodically knock people's hats off, or push elderly people down stairs, or shoot at passersby from the roof of some lofty tower, then I take myself to the sea. And so I bundled my few belongings, quit my lodgings in Manhattan, and made my way north.

In New Bedford I found myself lodged with a South Sea cannibal named Queequeg. He was a great, dark, muscular fellow covered from head to toe in tattoos and strange piercings, and every night he worshipped a little idol and smoked a big pipe. I did not so much mind sharing a bed with him—in fact I came to enjoy it—but I took pains to avoid him at mealtimes. I was stuck in New Bedford for several days, and we became good friends, Queequeg and I. I learned from my savage companion—who turned out not to be so savage as many a civilized fellow—I learned from him that cannibals are every bit as human as you or me, except that under certain circumstances they would eat us. Those of us who restrict the flesh we consume to that of quadrupeds are by no measure superior. I also learned that every religion will appear bizarre when scrutinized closely, and that Christianity should claim no superiority to Paganism simply because instead of worshipping animals we worship a dead young man nailed to a pair of sticks.

We finally made it to Nantucket and got ourselves signed onto the *Pequod,* which was set to embark on a three-year whaling voyage in just a few days. They were reluctant to sign Queequeg at first, despite the fact of his being an unerring harpooner, because the ship was run by a partnership of Quakers with a longstanding policy of *No Cannibals.* Queequeg threatened at first to take them to the Nantucket office of the Equal Employment Opportunity Commission, but when the ship's owner, one Captain Peleg, pointed out that there was no such thing, Queequeg simply promised not to eat anyone useful during the voyage, and to refrain while in Nantucket from dining upon any Quakers. This promise was deemed satisfactory.

We wanted to meet the captain before signing our contracts, but Peleg told us the captain had just returned from a three-year voyage. "And surely thou knowest that one captain is as good as another? Surely thou knowest better than to believe all the stories thou hearest? Surely thou disdainest all gossip? Who art thou to judge? And what art madness, anyway?" And so we signed, Queequeg and I; we signed on and hoped for the best.

The whale is a gigantic sea creature with a big head at one end and a great thick tail at the other. It is therefore a fish. Like us, the whale has warm blood and lungs; unlike most of us, the whale swims about in the watery depths of the ocean and breathes through the top of its head. There are different kinds of whales in different parts of the world. The most commonly hunted are the Right Whale of the North Atlantic and the Norway Right Whale. There are also Nearly Right Whales, Technically Right Whales, Slightly Erroneous Whales, Simply Wrong Whales, and a thousand other varieties besides. They have lots of blubber, which can be made into oil, and also ivory, and meat, and, some of them, ambergris. Ambergris is used as a skin lotion by many islanders of the South Seas, as an aphrodisiac by many Asians, as jewelry by some Australian aborigines, and an excellent plaque-fighting toothpaste in the Americas.

A few weeks later we were on our way, sailing southward in the Atlantic, and still we hadn't seen the captain. He had sneaked into his cabin in the middle of the night before we set sail, and had kept to his cabin ever since. We had heard stories about him: some of the men said that a whale had bit one of his legs off at the knee on his last voyage. They said he'd had an ivory replacement made for it. They said he'd gone mad. They said he had made a pact with Satan. They said he was Satan. They said to stand on fourteen if the dealer showed three. But none of this seemed consequential to Queequeg or myself, as the boat sailed along smoothly under the sensible guidance of First Mate Starbuck, Second Mate Stubb, and Third Mate Flask, onward toward our destiny, carrying us thither like a bowl of clams being carried to the chowder pot.

One afternoon after we'd made our way well into the sunny climes of the southern hemisphere, Captain Ahab finally made his first appearance. He was a great tree trunk of a man, with a stormy, brooding look. His black hair was wild and tangled, his dark beard thick and gnarled, his rough-worn face a crosshatching of scars, his neck a vertical column between his head and shoulders. His dark eyes shone with the manic light of a man possessed—which in fact, of course, he was.

"Everybody aft!" he thundered. "Down from the mastheads! Gather round, me hearties, gather round, me mates. Everybody aft!"

I thought at first he might be preparing to apologize for having been so inaccessible. Instead, he boomed out a question:

"What do ye do when ye see a whale, men?"

The crew cried out as one: "Sing out for him!"

"Good!" the captain said. "And what d'ye do next, men?"

"Lower away and after him!" they shouted in unison.

"And what tune is it ye pull to, men?"

" 'My Heart Belongs to Daddy'!" one fellow shouted.

There was a moment's awkward silence, until at last the rest of the crew boomed out as one:

"A Dead Whale or a Stove Boat!"

"Ay, me hearties, that's right! Now listen up: do ye see this here gold doubloon?"

"Aye, sir!" we shouted. (A few in back kept yelling, "Down in front!")

Captain Ahab eyed us sternly, appraising us with his cold, steely eyes. "Whosoever of ye raises me a white-headed whale with a wrinkled brow and a crooked jaw, whosoever of ye raises me that white-headed whale, with three holes punctured in his starboard flukes—listen up, me hearties—whosoever of ye raises me that white whale, that Moby Dick, whosoever of ye raises me that white-headed whale whose head, I say, is white—shall have this here gold doubloon!"

And a great cry of joy went forth from all the men at the prospect of this luminous golden incentive—all the men, that is, except for First Mate Starbuck.

"Was it not Moby Dick that got your leg, Captain?" he asked.

The crew fell silent. Ahab's face darkened. "Aye," he muttered, "so it was. It was Moby Dick dismasted me, Moby Dick that brought me to this dead stump I stand on now. Aye, aye! and I'll chase him round Good Hope, and round the Horn, and round the Norway Maelstrom, and round perdition's flames, and round a lot of other scary places before I give him up. And this is what ye have shipped for, men! To chase that white whale on both sides of land, and over all sides of the earth, till he spouts black blood and rolls fin out. Are ye with me, men?"

The men looked doubtful. One of the sailors held up his hand. "Does he really have to spout black blood and roll fin out, captain? Sometimes they roll the other way—would that count?"

"Just kill him! Now—*are ye with me, men?*"

"Aye!" cried the crew. "We chase the white whale! We hunt Moby Dick! We shackle our destinies to our captain's monomaniacal whims!"

And Ahab looked down upon Starbuck with a grim, triumphant smile.

"Excuse me, Captain," that good mate began, "but we didn't ship for Moby Dick. We shipped for spermaceti, and one whale's got about as much as the next. It does not sound as though you are hunting whales, *sir:* it sounds to me as though you are hunting vengeance."

Such storm clouds I have never seen as those that black-ened the captain's already forbidding expression, but his reply was icy calm. "I don't speak of vengeance," he said. "I'm not interested in vengeance, Mister Starbuck. I only want revenge."

With that the argument ended, and Starbuck wandered away from the rest of us to sulk and brood and contemplate mutiny, and perhaps brew some of his outstanding coffee. Ahab had some men bring up a special batch of Glog from the galley, and before letting us drink of it he performed a strange, elaborate ritual with Queequeg and the other har-pooners. It was a mysterious ritual involving their harpoons and their spears, which they touched to and rubbed against one another in rhythmic synchronicity, until at last it became too awkwardly homoerotic and they stopped. Then we all drank to the death of Moby Dick, not just once but twice, and then thrice. Thus were we consecrated in our unholy mission—consecrated and a little tipsy.

And so the *Pequod* sailed on, around Cape Horn and into the Pacific, across the Pacific and through the thousand coral-collared islands of the South Pacific, past Samoa and Fiji, past New Guinea and the Philippines, past an uncharted isle with seven stranded castaways, and on toward the South China Sea. Now and then a pod of whales was encountered, and the call would ring out from the masthead (or, more accurately, from a sailor perched upon the masthead, which rarely spoke itself): "Whalllll hooooo, thur sh'bloooow!" And the sleepy boat would rock to life, and the whaleboats would lower, and the four whaleboats of the *Pequod* would slice through the bellowing ocean in pursuit, one under the com-mand of Starbuck, one under Stubb, one under Flask, and one under the command of Ahab himself. And we would draw nigh upon the whales, and the harpooners would loose their spears, and perchance one would find its home, and the whale would thrash about, sometimes sounding into the depths, sometimes storming across the surface of the sea, sometimes doing elegant figure eights, the whaleboat loosing hundreds of yards of line, letting the leviathan exhaust itself in its struggle, and then, finally, drawing in the line, pulling the whaleboat to within yards of the wounded behemoth, and now, at last, loosing a torrent of spears at the creature's vulnerable spots—the eye, the spout, the tender spot behind the flukes, the testicles—and the struggle would end only as the beast's heart finally ruptured, and dark and bloody foam sprayed from its spouthole like pus from a well-squeezed pimple . . . and then whole days were spent in stripping and packing the flesh and oil of the slain creature, its blubber peeled off in great long swaths to be rendered into oil and stored away in barrels, its ambergris bottled, its ivory tickled.

Thus we sailed and sailed, catching some whales, missing others, Ahab's impatience growing every day we saw not the white whale, which was by far the majority of days. The captain was so feverishly gripped by his obsession that he even violated the first law of the sea, failing to stop and help a ship with a flat.

Then, at last, in the Sea of Japan, we finally caught sight of the great white whale: at last we beheld the legendary Moby Dick himself. We chased him several days, set out for him more than once, and always he eluded us. He was a master of disguise: several times we sailed right past him because we hadn't recognized him in his false mustache and glasses. On the third day we lowered for him, and Queequeg managed to sink a harpoon into his side. The whale rolled and pitched, and thrashed and leaped, and sounded and rose, and hopped and skipped, and cursed and spit, and churned the calm waters into a hellish foamy broth; with his mighty tail he splintered three of the whaleboats, my own among them; he dashed every spear and oar and harpoon to bits; he clobbered every sailor upside the head; such that only Ahab's boat, grim Ahab, unswerving Ahab, his boat alone still sat atop the waves.

We had been sorely whaled upon indeed, but the fierce determination on Ahab's brow made it clear that the struggle had just begun.

Whales are abundant in the mythology and legend of every culture the wide world has ever known. There are whales in the Bible, and there are whales in the Koran, and there are whales in Greek and Roman mythology, and there are whales in Shakespeare, and there are whales in philosophy, and there are whales in music, and there are whales in paintings by great artists, and there are whales in paintings by bad artists, and I have even drawn some whales myself, such as this one:

The *Pequod* sailed toward the scattered wreckage and gathered up those of us who had survived the whale's furious assault, while Ahab ordered his men to row their skiff to where he felt sure the leviathan would next breach. When lo!, Moby Dick breached, and not far from Ahab: whether guided by the unseen hand of destiny, or cast together by the impetuous hand of fate, or in fulfillment of some unknowable plan of the Creator, or simply to give my story an ending, the two were suddenly face-to-face. The beast's malignant eyes glittered above the waters, he lowered his head into the frothing foam (having first shut his eyes, which were perhaps sensitive to saltwater), and then the behemoth began moving malevolently toward the *Pequod*. First Mate Starbuck was not insensible of the damage the whale could do to the ship; he called out his orders and was obeyed, if not instantly then *very* quickly. But the *Pequod* was not meant for quick maneuvering, she was just a whale ship, and as whale ships customarily do business only with dead whales, and as dead whales are not as a rule very speedy, quickness is not a design factor. The boat turned slowly, too slowly, as the whale surged toward her, gathering momentum, plowing through the water so furiously as to send up a foamy spray as he swam, until at last he struck her amidships, and the boat shuddered, and the masts fell, and those aboard tripped and fell into one another, and in the galley the cook dropped the birthday cake he'd been preparing and fell face first into it, and the *Pequod* began to sink.

And now the great white whale turned; with cruel eye it beheld the last boat left upon the waves, Ahab's whaleboat. And Ahab stood in the bow, harpoon in hand, and stared back with wild defiance as the whale began moving toward him. The terrible blood feud would at last be settled, *mano a whalo.*

"Toward thee I roll," shouted Ahab, "though all-destroying but unconquering whale, to the last I grapple with thee; from hell's heart I stab at thee; for hate's sake I spit my last breath at thee. You stupid whale, I'll kick yer butt!"

Ahab loosed his spear with all the dark venom of his soul, and it flew straight to its mark. But the behemoth was upon the skiff now, and splintered the boat with a massive head butt, scattering her crew—all except Ahab, who had become tangled in the lines, and who was now dragged along behind Moby Dick as the whale sounded back down into the infernal depths where he dwelled. Down went the whale, and down, down, went Ahab with him. The other men were drowned in all the symbolism.

And by now the *Pequod* was so far sunk that only her masts were above the sea, and they were sinking fast. A vortex of swirling waters whirled around the boat, creating a whirlpool, sucking everything into its voracious center, everything that bobbed atop the waters, and even I was being drawn inexorably into the center, even I seemed consigned to a watery death, when just at the very last moment Queequeg's airtight coffin popped up from the depths beside me, and became my lifeboat.

Did I tell you Queequeg had built himself an airtight coffin? I meant to.

—The End—

Crime and Punishment

by Fyodor Dostoyevsky

(1866)

People with new ideas, people with the faintest capacity for saying something *new*, are extremely few in number, extraordinarily so, in fact. . . . The vast mass of mankind is mere material, and only exists in order by some great effort, by some mysterious process, by means of some crossing of races and stocks, to bring into the world at last perhaps one man out of a thousand with a spark of independence. One in ten thousand perhaps—I speak roughly, approximately—is born with some independence, and with still greater independence one in a hundred thousand. The man of genius is one of millions, and the great geniuses, the crown of humanity, appear on earth perhaps one in many thousand millions. . . .

Crime and Punishment *was published in 1866, in a turbulent Russia nothing like the stable and prosperous Russia of today. The tsars of Russia were among the most reactionary of Western Civilization's heads of state, and the czars were even worse. Popular discontent had been rising throughout the nineteenth century, and in an effort to stem the tide of impending revolt the tsar had even gone so far as to declare the Emancipation of the Surf in 1861. Unfortunately this radical measure engendered little support, as there were very few surfers in Russia at the time, and they weren't interested in politics anyway.*

Fiodor Dostoievski had always been a devoutly pious Russian Orthodox Catholic, and had always been loyal to the tsar. He was therefore arrested, convicted of treason, and sentenced to death by firing squad and chickens. Brought to stand before an open grave and then blindfolded, Dostoievski awaited his death. A shot rang out. He fell down, mortally wounded, and the chickens finished him off.

Standing beside him, however, was Fyodor Dostoyevsky, who had also always been a devoutly pious Russian Orthodox Catholic and loyal to the tsar, and was therefore also awaiting execution. Suddenly a messenger arrived from the Winter Palace: it had all been a nutty mix-up! Dostoyevsky was spared his life, and merely exiled to Siberia for ten years.

He fell in love and got married during his exile, but the whole expe-
rience had made such a wreck of him that he had inadvertently become
a brooding Russian genius. This surprised everyone, as studies had
repeatedly demonstrated that Russia already had more than her share of
brooding geniuses. But as everyone liked Fyodor, and as he was able to
disarm his most serious critics with his broad and brilliant repertoire of
fart jokes, he was allowed to write more Great Nineteenth-Century
Russian Novels despite the fact that the quota had been reached decades
earlier.

On an exceptionally hot evening early in July a young
man came out of the garret in which he lodged in S. Place
and walked slowly, as though in hesitation, toward K. Bridge.
He was an extremely handsome young student, dressed
entirely in rags. Where his rags had worn through he had
apparently patched them with leaves. The soles of his boots
were held in place by loops of frayed twine. He wore a small
cardboard box for a hat.

"I'll do it," he muttered to himself, "can I really do it?
Napoleon could have done it. I'll do it!"

But he couldn't do it, not really, not yet. His lips trembled,
his eyes flashed. His pale features flushed. Was he really capable of doing it? *That?* He had turned it over in his mind time
after time in the grimy solitude of his room, had examined it
from every angle, but he still wasn't sure if he could go
through with it. Could he?

He stopped in the middle of the K. Bridge and stepped
aside to make room for an old woman struggling to climb up
the railing. Her eyes were shining and feverish (and very hard
to see, as she had her back to him), but he heard her coarsely
mumbling her prayers. She jumped into the Neva and
drowned, and he resumed walking.

"Yes," he thought, "an old woman jumps to her death, and
it means nothing, it changes nothing. H'm . . . Perhaps—but
then . . . Hang it!" His thoughts were all in a whirl, for he had

once been a student, and he had studied all the new philosophies, and he was Russian. It was all too confusing.

He suddenly found himself standing before the door to an apartment building. "Here I am," he thought, and indeed, there he was. He entered the building, and hurried up two flights of stairs to the cramped top floor. He stood before the impoverished door. "Yes," he thought, "yes, I *can* do it; I *will* do it."

He turned the knob and swung the door open. Sitting behind a desk piled high with books and papers, in the midst of all the filth and squalor of the garret, was Razumihin, his old schoolmate.

Razumihin looked up at him, startled at first, but relaxing when he recognized Raskolnikov. Razumihin was one of the few university students who hadn't put a restraining order on him. "Rodya Sonovabich! I haven't seen you in over a year! You were always so strangely reclusive and unapproachable at university! But look at you—your eyes are shining, your lips are trembling, your face is pale and twisted into a terrible and grim visage of something like determined despair. I thought you'd given up on philosophy."

Raskolnikov's trembling redoubled, his thoughts crowded in upon him in a frenzied jumble: could he do it? *That?* Was *it* really possible?

"I need a job," Raskolnikov said, shaking violently. Sweat streamed down his face. His hair glistened. His eyes shook.

"Well," Razumihin said, "certainly, certainly, I could use some help on some German translations. . . ."

Suddenly Raskolnikov recoiled. He shook his head and moaned a low, agonized groan, then hurried back out of the apartment, back down the stairs, back into the stifling and oppressive heat of the St. Petersburg streets, which were as stifling and oppressive as everything else in Russia, which was great and yearned to be free.

"I knew it," Raskolnikov thought. "I knew I couldn't do it."

It was settled, then. He would have to kill the old lady.

. . .

He went back to his flat that night and slept uneasily, twitching and moaning in his sleep, and dreaming fantastic dreams full of wild symbolism. In one of them he was back in the provincial town of H., where he'd grown up. He was a child again. He was walking down a dusty country road with his father. There was a commotion in the road ahead of them, in front of a tavern. A drunken peasant was standing in the middle of the road, yelling at his horse, and a crowd of equally drunken peasant men and long-suffering but noble-hearted Russian prostitutes spilled out of the tavern to watch him.

"Stupid horse!" cried the man. "I said dance!"

The horse, who was poor and suffering, and old and loyal, and had never asked anyone for anything in his life, stared back at his master with a look of sad bewilderment.

"We told you, Mikolka: you'll never get that old nag to dance!"

"Dance!" Mikolka cried in a paroxysm of rage. "I tell you to dance, dance, dance!"

There were laughs and titters from the crowd, and these only served to enrage Mikolka. "You stupid horse! You worthless, vile nag! Stupid! You're stupid, you're ugly, and as for your breath—! I despise you!"

"Mikolka, Mikolka, you'll wound her self-esteem!"

But Mikolka would not listen, and continued to harass the horse, and insult its intelligence and appearance, and betray the years of amicable coexistence they had shared, and in other ways so torment the horse that eventually it lowered itself to the ground and died of a broken heart.

Little Raskolnikov was weeping, hysterical.

"Never mind," his father said, pulling him along, "they're sad and tragic people, these peasants. Their sorrow is endless. They're only cruel because life has been cruel to them. Remember that we are not much better than common peasants ourselves, although we do speak a little French, *n'est-ce pas?*"

Raskolnikov woke up. Tears were streaming down his face.

O, Russia, Russia, Russia!

The concierge, Nastyassy, was standing in his doorway.

"Upon my soul! Are you going to sleep all day, then?" Nastyassy was of that bright and playful disposition that was inexplicably found so often in the poor and oppressed Russian working class, whose courage and resilience in the face of utter hopelessness was a testament to either man's essential optimism or his invincible stupidity. Probably both.

"Leave me alone," Raskolnikov snapped.

"Did someone wake up on the wrong side of the lumpy cot this morning?"

"Why must you torment me?—*leave me!*"

"I'll leave you," Nastyassy chirped, "but I thought you'd want to see this letter that arrived a week ago from your loving and long-suffering Russian mother." She handed him the letter and left.

Raskolnikov read the letter with a trembling hand:

My dearest Rodya

Your sister Dunya and I remain here in the provinces, and I would never trouble you with news of our bitter disappointments, or how we work ourselves to the bone in a noble sacrifice for your education, or how we worry ourselves sick about you. We suffer gladly in silence. We are just a poor but honest Russian family after all, whose tender compassion may someday set an example for you, but for the time being probably appears comically trite. I'm only writing to tell you that Dunya was unfairly disgraced by the wicked landowner Svidrigaïlov, who had attempted to seduce her on account of her ravishing beauty. Fortunately his wife, Marfa Petrovna, eventually realized she had misunderstood everything, and that it had actually been her husband's misconduct, not our precious Dunya's. Marfa Petrovna felt so badly about the confusion that she found a wealthy man to marry Dunya. He is Marfa Petrovna's cousin, Pyotr Pumpkyneatrovich Luzhin. He is quite wealthy and must therefore be wonderful and loving deep down, for otherwise God would not have let him have so much money. He has mostly been rude and violent so far, but that is only to be expected of a bridegroom. I promise he is not the browbeating, arrogant, ignorant and miserly type you might have feared Dunya would marry in order to gain enough money to ensure our livelihood and the continuation of your education. He will be coming to St. Petersburg to discuss the arrangements with you, because Dunya would not agree to marry him until you had approved the match. He has been kind enough to pay for our journey to St. Petersburg, although we will be arriving somewhat later than him as we will be travelling on the cargo train in a large box.

All my love,
Worried sick,
Pulcheria Melancholovna Raskolnikov
(Your mother)

"Well," Raskolnikov thought, "so that's how it is, they're going to sacrifice themselves for me, are they? They cannot—they must not! It is loathsome, I will not allow it!—... But can I really do *it*? Yes, yes, I must, it is time."

He put on his rags and leaves and his cardboard hat. He snuck into the first-floor tenant's apartment and stole the axe from under his sofa, tucking it into a special axe holster he had sewn into the lining of his overcoat.

Then he wandered out into the sweltering streets, distracted and confused. Rivulets of sweat streamed down his face again, perhaps because he was wearing an overcoat in July. As he passed the high walls of a certain bourgeois home, a dark figure climbed over the wall into the street and scurried away hurriedly; from within the house, someone was screaming, *"Parricide! Parricide!"*

"Ah, Russia!" Raskolnikov thought. "Wherefore, wherefore? You are like a great troika rumbling across the steppe, heedlessly driven by a dimwitted drunk, demolishing everything in your path—the world stands back and beholds your terrible coming: shall they step aside? or will they be crushed beneath your wheels? or will they just keep their distance until you sober up? O, Russia, Russia, Russia!"

When he was done thinking about Russia and how tragically mixed up she was, he wandered around the city some more, wondering what he would have done if he were Napoleon. Finally it was twilight. It was time to do *it*.

He stole quickly through the lobby and climbed four flights of steps to the fourth floor, since in Russia, as in many other parts of the world, the first floor was actually on the second floor, so that what they called the fourth floor was really the fifth. On the third floor, which in some countries might have been called the fourth, he noticed some workmen painting an empty apartment. It was the one directly under *hers*. "So, no one lives beneath her? So much the better! If, that is, I were actually to carry out my plan, which perhaps I won't. Won't I? Oh, I must! Mustn't I, though? Ach! Hang it!" His lip trembled and his heart beat violently. He knocked upon the door.

"Yes?" came the old woman's voice.

"It's Rodyon Sonovabich Raskolnikov, Alyona Miserovna!"

The door opened a crack, and the pawnbroker's haggard face peeped through. "Ah, yes," she muttered, letting him in, "the poor young former student with the trembling lips and palpitating heart. You're here to redeem your pledge?"

"No," Raskolnikov said, "I . . . I'm afraid I need more. More time, and—yes, certainly, and more money . . . If you please, Alyona Miserovna, I have . . . it's in my coat pocket here, if I can find it. . . ." His face flushed and his teeth were chattering. His hand trembled as he dug through his pocket. His pancreas fluttered violently. "Yes, here it is: I'd like to pawn this cigarette case, and pay the interest on the watch I brought three weeks ago."

The old woman snatched the "pledge" away from him greedily. It was in quotes because in fact it was only a piece of wood wrapped in tissue paper. Raskolnikov had wrapped it very tightly because he knew the old woman had terrible rheumatism: while she struggled to unwrap it, he withdrew the axe from under his coat, raised it over her head, and brought its blunt end smashing down on her skull. It made a squishy cracking sound.

"Ow," she said, then crumpled to the floor.

Raskolnikov struck what was left of her skull a few more times with the axe, then stopped what he was doing and stared down at her.

"She's dead," he thought, "she was alive a moment ago, and now she's dead. I did that . . . Have I really done it? Well—who else, I'd like to know? It's not as though it's crowded in here! Yes, she's certainly dead. Is that her ear, or . . . That must be her nose, her ear is over . . . Good Heavens! What have I done?" A moment passed. "That's right, now I remember, I killed her. Napoleon would have done the same thing. Very good. I mustn't let these emotions . . . But I knew this would happen, and yet—but wait! What's that? I hear footsteps!"

Indeed, he had no sooner hidden himself behind the front door, which he had foolishly left open, than in came the spinster's breathtakingly stupid sister, Lizaveta Miserovna.

"Alyona," said Lizaveta, "Alyona, are you all right? What happened to your head, Alyona? Merciful Heavens, are those your brains? Shall I gather them in a bucket, Alyona?"

Raskolnikov leaped out of his hiding place and brought

the axe down on Lizaveta's head, cutting it in half. Then he ran around the room, grabbed whatever valuables he could find, and fled.

He walked through the mists of the St. Petersburg night in a daze. "I've done it," he told himself repeatedly, and then, "But have I really done it?" His eyes were glassy with distraction, his tongue cleaved to the roof of his mouth, his toenails tingled. "I suppose I've done it," he thought.

Suddenly he stopped in his tracks. "What have I done?" he wondered rhetorically, although he knew perfectly well that he had just killed two Russian women with an axe. It was more than he could bear. He was becoming unhinged. He dashed into the nearest tavern.

A poor young girl, of no more than thirteen years, was playing the balalaika and singing sad, sweet Russian songs about how full of suffering life was, but how we all had our crosses to bear and that if we all did our best maybe we'd end up in heaven with the angels, all our sins forgiven.

A drunken fellow named Marmelade collared Raskolnikov and confessed that he'd drunk so much he'd brought poverty and shame upon his family, forcing his eldest daughter, Sonya, into prostitution. His wife was dying of tuberculosis and their three other children, the oldest of whom was ten, wouldn't be able to prostitute themselves for another two or three years.

Raskolnikov took pity on Marmelade and helped the staggering drunk back to his house, where the landlady was screaming at his wife and the children were stewing in filth and the cockroaches had taken the best corner of the decrepit room for themselves.

"Ah," thought Raskolnikov, "yes, yes, it's all so terrible, so honest, so Russian, so completely irrelevant."

And he went back out to wander in the streets some more, and he buried the valuables he'd stolen under a big rock somewhere, and he washed the blood off the toes of his boots and the lining of his overcoat, and he returned the axe to its place beneath the couch of the first-floor tenant, and then he went up to his room and crawled into bed and slept a fitful, nightmarish sleep.

He woke up in a delirium. Nastyassy stood in his doorway.

"You've been summoned by the police," she giggled.

"Already?" Raskolnikov cried. "Very well," he thought, "they've no evidence, nothing at all to pin on me, and after all—after all, I had every right! Yes! I am no ordinary man—I'm extraordinary! Their petty morality means nothing to me! I am immune to their bourgeois prejudices! I am—*Napoleonic!*"

"Excuse me," he said to Nastyassy, "I need to get dressed."

Nastyassy left the room.

The summons had nothing to do with the murder, however, but rather Raskolnikov's having failed to pay rent for the last two years. While he argued with one policeman, another entered the room. "Say," he said, "have you heard about the two old ladies that got axed to death last night?" Raskolnikov felt weak. The room swirled around him. He clutched at the arms of his chair for support. Unfortunately it was one of those chairs without arms, and he fell to the floor in a dead faint.

When he woke up, of course, everyone laughed about what a funny coincidence it had been, his passing out at the exact moment that the one officer had mentioned the murder of the old women and everything, and in a burst of good Russian conviviality they released Raskolnikov, suggesting only that he ask himself how he might feel if he had rented an apartment to someone who kept forgetting to pay rent. It wouldn't feel very nice, would it?

Back on the streets, Raskolnikov began a slow downward

spiral into madness. It took several long and torturous days. His mother and sister appeared and fretted over him and urged him to get more fiber in his diet and begged him to let them sacrifice their own happiness for his. Luzhin appeared and begged his permission to marry Dunya. Razumihin appeared and felt sure he could help if only Raskolnikov would *let him* help, and went so far as to fall in love with Dunya. Svidrigaïlov appeared and told him ghost stories and confessed to pedophilia and swore he wouldn't seduce another child if only he could marry Dunya. Marmelade was run over by a coach and died before he had a chance to think about marrying Dunya. Raskolnikov himself fell in love with Marmelade's daughter, Sonya, because she was a prostitute and therefore noble and pure of heart. He tried to help Sonya cope as her mother went mad in the final stages of TB, sold her other children to the circus, and died. And so on and so forth, all of it very dark and sorrowful and tragic and Russian.

And moving through all of these events, mysteriously if awkwardly, cunningly if stupidly, was Razumihin's distant cousin, the new police inspector, Porfiry Columbovich. Raskolnikov could never tell if Porfiry suspected him or not. Sometimes the inspector was friendly; sometimes he was aloof. Sometimes he all but accused Raskolnikov directly; sometimes he told him jokes about Mrs. Porfiry Columbovich. Raskolnikov considered him a vulgar knave.

Of course, Raskolnikov considered everyone a vulgar knave (except Napoleon).

One night Raskolnikov went to Sonya's room, her shameful prostitute's room where she lived alone with her heart of gold, and with feverish eyes and quivering ears he begged her to read him the story of Lazarus from the New Testament.

Her eyes shining, her voice trembling with emotion, her calves twitching, she read from the fourth gospel:

" 'Get up,' Jesus said, and Lazarus got up. 'See?' said Jesus. And no one could believe it, and they were greatly mystified. And Jesus said, 'If you people would just *listen* once in a while, and pay some *attention,* you wouldn't keep dying and I wouldn't have to raise you from the dead.' And the people listened to him from that day forward; they listened really, really carefully."

Raskolnikov had begun weeping as soon as she had started to read; now he lay his head in Sonya's lap and sobbed as he told her all he had done, and she wept with him, and it was cleansing. Not literally, but spiritually—although the tears did wash away little streaks of filth from their faces. He was stirred to the depths, as if he were a big kettle of stew and she were a big wooden spoon.

She promised to follow him to Siberia.

Another evening, toward the end of the novel, Porfiry Columbovich found Raskolnikov alone in his garret.

"I know you did it," Porfiry said, "and I know you're going to turn yourself in before I'm forced to have you arrested. It will be better for you if you confess—you'll almost certainly get time off for having a complex and troubled Russian soul corrupted by the confused and confusing *zeitgeist* of our era. It's a strange time. We are all of us poor, and accursed, and corrupt, and vile; we wrap ourselves tightly in the mantle of our own suffering; we're hungry, we're starving, we endure one misfortune after another, we don't expect anything good ever to come of it, and yet we're full of pity, sometimes, and sometimes we're just amused; we're cruel, like children, we're quick to react, we're always throwing ourselves off bridges or getting run over by horses or marrying drunks or turning to prostitution, and the so-called worst among us have the noblest of motives, while the so-called nobles have the worst of motives, and the intellectuals are busy spewing nonsense, and the wealthy care for nothing but their wealth. Everyone loves God, but everyone doubts God, because everyone fears God; our Russian God is like the Hebrew God; sorrowful but terrible. Everyone is a shyster. Everyone drinks. Everyone is bawdy. Everyone accepts things as they are, but no one can stand it even a moment longer. And we've all got these crazy Russian names."

"Yes," said Raskolnikov. "Yes, you're right, of course. I will surrender. I will suffer for my crime."

"Well then," said Porfiry.

"Well," said Raskolnikov.

And neither of them knew what else to say, because it was the end of the whole long, dark, sorrowful Russian novel, and they both felt kind of awkward.

—The End—

The Picture of Dorian Gray

by Oscar Wilde

(1890)

I am jealous of everything whose beauty does not die. I am jealous of the portrait you have painted of me. Why should it keep what I must lose? Every moment that passes takes something from me, and gives something to it. Oh, if it were only the other way! If the picture would change, and I could be always what I am now! Why did you paint it? It will mock me some day—mock me horribly!

By the end of the nineteenth century Great Britain had become almost entirely Victorian, and England quickly followed suit. The Victorian era was principally remarkable for its suppression of sex, which was facilitated by the unprecedented population explosion of the age. As an Irish citizen, Oscar Wilde was not properly trained in Victorianism, and this caused him considerable trouble in London.

Born in Dublin in 1854, Wilde was a brilliant, remarkable, and contradictory man who, after a long and stellar career producing extraordinary literature and memorable quotes, was sentenced to prison for "acts of gross indecency with other mail persons." It was a surprising sentence, as Wilde had never actually worked in the postal service, but there was no appeal. He served his time in a special prison for writers, whose inmates were forced to read bad books: the notorious Reading Gaol (in English, "Reading Jail").

Scholars have debated for decades what those acts of gross indecency may have been, and although the question may never be answered to anyone's satisfaction, they appear to be having a grand old time discussing it.

The studio was filled with the rich odour of roses, and when the light summer wind stirred amidst the trees of the garden, there came through the open door the heavy scent of the lilac, or the more delicate perfume of the pink-flowering thorn, or the odour of some other smelly plant. Lord Henry Wotton reclined languorously on a divan of Persian saddle-bags, smoking innumerable cigarettes, some of them opium-tainted, as was his fashion. He was gazing with heavy-lidded pleasure at a painting his friend Basil Hallward had been working on.

"Really, Basil, it's captivating. Who is this beautiful youth? Those golden curls, those dreamy blue eyes, those luscious ruby lips, those extraordinary ears . . . You've done him a great disservice painting him so well: real beauty, like real cheese, is spoiled when it knows itself."

"Never mind who it is," Basil replied. Basil had a strong and rugged face, dark, piercing eyes, and hair as black as coal at midnight, on a starless night. Maybe blacker. It was very black. "I tell you, Harry, it is the finest work I have ever done. I feel differently about this painting than any painting I have ever painted before."

"Yes," drawled Lord Henry, stroking his pointed brown beard, "yes, you must have it shown at all the galleries. The Academy, the Grosvenor, the Peanut. . . . All art is idiotic, of course, and all galleries are tedious, but not nearly as tedious as the men and women who attend them. They are insufferable. I have always said there is nothing as vulgar as the insufferable; except, perhaps, for the sufferable."

"Oh, Harry!" cried Basil, wiping the tears of laughter from his eyes, "that cynical wit just slays me! But I cannot show this painting at any gallery: it is too close to me, too precious. I have put too much of myself into it, and I cannot let that be seen. As an artist, it is vital that I conceal my finest work."

"I should like to meet the boy," Lord Henry said.

"You will not meet him," Basil said abruptly, his face flushing. "He is mine. He has brought joy and light back into my life. He is my sunshine, my only sunshine, he makes me happy when skies are gray. You would corrupt him; I can't allow that. You must not take my sunshine away."

"My dear Basil," Lord Henry began, "I am incapable of corruption." He smiled significantly, and blew several smoke rings, watching them drift toward the skylight in lazy, opium-befuddled torpor. "Corruption is born of good intentions," he continued. "I have no good intentions."

Basil frowned. "Stop posing, Harry. You forget how long I've known you. You may be wicked, depraved, immoral, and licentious, but you aren't evil. And I don't believe for a moment that all your intentions are wicked."

"It's true," Basil agreed, "not all my intentions are wicked: only the pleasant ones. But life is far too short for good intentions. I have always said that good intentions pave the road to tedium, and that I should rather spend twenty pounds on charity than twenty minutes in tedium. Now tell me how you met this delightful Adonis."

"Very well," said Basil, "but come, let's step into the garden." Lord Henry rose and the two men stepped out into the radiant sunshine. They sat on a low stone bench by some flowery bushes that smelled good. "I met him at one of Lady Brandon's crushes. I was about to go home, when suddenly I felt that I was being watched. I turned halfway around, or perhaps two-thirds of the way—call it three-fifths—and there he was, staring at me from across the room! With one look at his face I knew I had to flee this young man. His beauty was more than I could bear."

"You fell in love with him?"

"And what is that supposed to imply?"

"Aren't you . . . ?"

"Good lord, Harry! Of course not. I'm an impeccably repressed Victorian gentleman."

"And yet you paint only young boys."

"I was only transfixed by his impossible aesthetic perfection. Kindly allow me to finish my story. I rushed for the door, but Lady Brandon blocked my path. 'Basil Hallward!' she squealed. 'You're not leaving, are you? There's someone you must meet before you leave. His mother and I are absolutely inseparable. Come, come, I want you to meet Dorian Gray—' "

"Ha!" cried Lord Henry, emphasizing his excitement by tapping the pointed toe of one tasselled patent leather shoe with the ivory tip of his licorice cane. "So that's his name! You didn't want to tell me his name, but I got it! I got it! Yes! Ha!"

A look of inconsolable sadness darkened Basil's face. "I beg you," he said without looking up, "I beg you in the name of our many years of friendship, Lord Henry, I beg you not to look for Dorian Gray. I beg you: leave him to me. Let him be. He is everything to me. He is more than my sunshine. He is my groovy little booby. Please, stay away from him."

"Well," sighed Lord Henry, "If it means that much to you . . ."

Suddenly the butler stepped into the garden. "Mr. Dorian Gray is in the studio, sir."

Basil winced.

"Excellent!" cried Lord Henry.

"Tell him I'll be just a moment," Basil said to the butler. When the butler entered the house, Basil turned to Lord Henry. "I beg of you," he begged, "I implore you," he implored, "I . . . I beseech you: do not spoil him. Do not corrupt him."

"Pfah!" laughed Lord Henry, rising, and he led his wretched friend into the house.

Dorian had already struck his pose by the time they entered the studio.

"This is Lord Henry Wotton," Basil said. "He's an old friend of mine from our Oxford days. Lord Henry, Dorian Gay. Beg pardon: Dorian *Gray*."

"People always make that mistake," Dorian said softly. "I'm rather used to it."

Lord Henry smiled. "My aunt has spoken of you often," he said.

"Ah," Dorian said. "I am afraid I am in Lady Agatha's black books at the moment."

"Then we have something in common," cried Lord Henry. "It is fine to have things in common. The only thing finer is not to have things in common. I have always said that nothing unites people like the things that unite them, except perhaps those things that divide them."

Dorian laughed so hard he blew milk out his nose, which was unusual in that he had not been drinking any milk. "You're clever and captivating," he said. "Basil didn't tell me he had any clever and captivating friends."

"Because I don't," Basil growled.

"Basil is bitter because he wanted to keep you to himself," Lord Henry observed. "He is always trying to keep the best things from his friends. He's quite selfish that way. I am not at all selfish. Selfishness is vulgar. The only thing more vulgar than selfishness is unselfishness. It has always been my belief that the rain in Spain stays mainly in the plain."

"Ah!" cried Dorian, "It's true! And in Hartford, Hereford, and Hampshire, hurricanes hardly happen! Basil, why didn't you tell me you had a friend who could open my eyes to the bejewelled splendor of the world?"

"Because I don't," Basil growled, sorting through his brushes. "But I'm very nearly done with the portrait. Indeed, this shall be your last sitting."

As Basil worked on the portrait, Dorian held his pose and Lord Henry reclined beside him, watching attentively.

"You are very fortunate to be so beautiful," said Lord Henry, "for Beauty is the greatest thing in the world. And you also have youth. Youth is good too. Having them both together is quite extraordinary: Beauty and Youth together are something only beautiful young people have. The world will bow down before you. Indeed, even better, it will bend over before you. There is nothing you cannot do or have. You are Superman."

A strange glow illuminated Dorian's features. Basil noticed it; his own face lit up, and he began painting furiously.

"Do you really think so?" fished Dorian.

"I know so," said Lord Henry. "But make good use of it, for Age will conquer you, will devour your Youth, will assault your Beauty, and you'll be ugly and old like the rest of us. Time is a terrible monster, like a werewolf or a vampire: it sucks the essence out of us and leaves us hideously deformed, monsters that must go out into the night and suck the blood out of innocent victims."

A curious expression crossed Dorian's face, a strange recognition, as though he were suddenly realizing something important that he hadn't previously realized. He stayed like that for five minutes, and no one spoke, until finally Basil cried:

"Done!"

Lord Henry and Dorian walked over to the easel to look at the portrait.

"Extraordinary," said Lord Henry.

"It is the finest thing I have ever done in my life," said Basil. "It was already good, but then in those last five minutes I captured something of that curious expression on Dorian's face. . . . I feel as if I have captured his very soul on this canvas!"

"No!" cried Dorian. "No, it's not fair! This portrait is going to stay young and beautiful forever, and I'm going to get old and ugly. I wish it were the other way around! I wish it were the other way around! I wish it were the other way around!" Thunder crackled, lightning flashed, haunting music swelled, and the air became charged with a supernatural electricity.

"Well," said Basil, "it's your painting, Dorian. I'll send it to you once it dries."

"Why don't you join me for dinner and come to the ballet with me tonight?" asked Lord Henry.

"I should love to!" Dorian exclaimed. "I feel a sudden surge of power, a potent libidinous pulsing deep within me, strange stirrings—I feel capable of anything! Yes, dinner and a ballet! London shall bend over before me! Yes!"

Dorian left the room in a flurry of giddy excitement.

Lord Henry smiled at Basil. "See you soon," he said, and he swished hurriedly after Dorian.

Basil sat down and wept, for Basil could not leave.

Several weeks later Dorian fell in love with the charming young lead actress of a small and otherwise mediocre theatre company. Her name was Sibyl Vane. He loved her completely and without abandon. She was a genius on stage, and Dorian never missed one of her shows. She fell in love with him every bit as violently as he had with her. The girl's mother disapproved only until she learned that Dorian was rich. Her brother vowed to kill anyone who brought unhappiness to his sister, then sailed off for Australia to await a later chapter.

At last Dorian proposed to her, and she accepted. In his feverish happiness, he invited Basil and Lord Henry to join him at the theatre and meet the beautiful genius that would soon be his wife. On this night, however, her acting was shallow and artificial. Her movements were awkward and contrived. She forgot her lines and bumped into the furniture. The audience pelted her with rotten tomatoes, cabbages, and eggs. Lord Henry and Basil left the theatre. Dorian was humiliated. He stormed into the dressing room after the show.

"My beloved!" Sibyl cried, rushing to him. "Did you see how badly I performed? It's because now that I know what real life is, real life and real love, I suddenly see how shallow and unreal are those foolish parts I play."

"You have humiliated me in front of my friends," Dorian said. "That was unpleasant. You have lost your talent, and I no longer love you. You're a bad actress, and your makeup is atrocious. Good-bye."

He turned and left the startled and devastated girl behind.

. . .

When he got home he decided to lift his spirits by admiring his portrait for a while. When he sat in front of it, however, he froze in horror: the lower lip in the portrait was curled cruelly, with hideous self-satisfaction, suggesting such wickedness as might be seen on the face of a man who had been vain enough to sever relations with the woman he loved simply because she hadn't impressed his friends.

He looked in a mirror: no such cruelty marred his own mouth. His face was radiant and lovely as ever. He kissed himself—deeply, longingly—then glanced back at the portrait and was horrified again. There was no denying the grotesque cruelty of that curled lip.

Dorian realized all at once what had happened: his wish, uttered on a momentary whim, had come true: the portrait had recorded his wickedness to Sibyl while his own face had remained blissfully unmarred.

"Cool," he said.

He decided to write Sibyl an apology, and beg her to take him back and marry him. At about that time Lord Henry arrived. Dorian told him how he had broken off the engagement, and how he intended to beg her forgiveness.

"She cannot forgive you, Dorian," Lord Henry said. "She has killed herself."

"Ah," Dorian said, "then my repentance is in Vane." He lowered himself into the Louis Quatorze armchair that he had had reupholstered with an intricate Persian threadwork of spun shark hair. "It's a pity," he said.

"Yes," said Lord Henry. "Suicide is always a pity. It is the opiate of the masses. I have always said that I should sooner kill myself than be caught committing suicide. I hope you won't be implicated in any of it."

"No," Dorian said, "no, I was careful never to tell her my name or where I lived, despite the fact that we were going to be married, on the off chance that something like this might happen. She only knew me as Prince Charming."

"You're very prudent," Lord Henry observed. "I have always said that being prudent in love is like balancing a tumbler of vermouth on the end of one's nose while waltzing a chimpanzee: it's a waste of vermouth, and it irritates the monkey!"

"I don't understand," Dorian sighed.

"Neither do I!" cried Lord Henry, "I make it a point never to understand myself. I assure you if I ever understood myself I should stop speaking at once!" And the two men laughed pleasantly and went to see a ballet.

Eighteen years went by. Dorian went through a number of passions, some of them for months, some for years. He sought to experience everything. He threw himself completely into music during one period, and collected and learned to play strange and exotic instruments, many of which had never before been seen in Europe: the Diddlebum of Tanzania, for example, with its aching, lonesome, wryly disappointed chords; the Scruttlecock of Malay aborigines, which was played by blowing through one's ear; the Boom-Boom drums of Outer Mongolia, which turned out not to be drums after all, but powerful explosives, and which cost Dorian half of his fine staff. When he exhausted music he moved on to jewels, studying and collecting gems and stones from every quarter of the earth; then he moved on to tapestries, then religious vestments, then belly button lint—he astonished his peers by spending £200,000 on a thimbleful of lint that had been plucked from the belly button of Genghis Khan on the day he took Damascus, and which had been preserved through the centuries by a secret sect of Tatar mystics. From enthusiasm to enthusiasm he bounded, like a dog in a park running from tree to tree and making his golden mark on each of them as if to say, "Been there, done that."

• • •

It was on the ninth of November, the eve of his thirty-eighth birthday, that Dorian chanced to bump into Basil Hallward just outside his house. Basil said he had been waiting for Dorian nearly an hour, and had very nearly given up on him. He was quite pleased not to have missed him: he was on his way to Paris for six months, but he had felt he must have a word with Dorian before he left. Dorian was irritated, for Basil was always irritating, but he invited him in.

They stood in the den, and Dorian poured each of them a drink, not wanting to wake the servants.

"I must tell you, Dorian," Basil began, "if only for the sake of our old friendship, I must tell you that people are saying atrocious things about you behind your back. Listen to me, Dorian! I've had to defend you from the most infamous accusations on more than one occasion. Why, the things Lord Halibut blames you with in regard to his son—if I thought for a moment you were capable of such . . . ! And yet I have seen with my own eyes how the Earl of Snotshire leaves any room you enter. I have seen Lady Gristle faint at your approach—twice! I have heard stories about you that if I believed for one moment they were true I should never call you my friend again, and would indeed be more likely to sneak in upon you as you slept, drive a stake through your heart, and cut off your head."

"And you wanted to tell me this because . . . ?"

"Because you must clear yourself of this dark talk, Dorian!"

Dorian smiled warmly at Basil. "That isn't why you've come, is it? You want to hear me deny all those terrible rumours."

"It would help to hear your side of things."

"On which account?"

"On all of them, of course. The most serious ones, at least: do you know there are at least three families, three prominent families that hold you accountable for . . . And poor Lord Halibut . . . His only son . . . ! And the tales of you being seen in strange places, with strange people, doing unspeakable things—you can't imagine what people think you did to Professor Plum, with a candlestick, in the drawing room ... But then I look at you, with your fresh, innocent face, and of course I can't believe a word of it."

A sudden fancy turned in Dorian's mind. "Would you like to know the absolute truth of everything?" he asked. "I shall show you. I have kept a record of it all."

And so Dorian lit one of the servants' lamps and led his old friend up the stairs, quietly, so as not to waken the servants—whom he was always concerned about not waking, being the thoughtful sort of aristocrat that he was—and into the secret upstairs room in which the portrait hung behind a thick curtain. He set the lamp on a table and faced Basil. "It was your doing," he said, "and so I share the secret with you. No one else shall ever know of it."

With that he pulled back the curtain, and said, "Here! Here! It is the beating of this hideous heart!"

Basil cried aloud at the horrible face that grinned back at him from the canvas.

"It can't be!" he moaned, falling to his knees, "It can't be! Dorian, no! Pray with me! Pray! It's not too late, you can change, Dorian! Today is the first day of the rest of your life! There's no time like the present! Neither a borrower nor a lender be! Oh, wretched creature, wretched creature! Open your heart, Dorian, it is never too late to—"

It was at about this moment that Dorian noticed the knife gleaming conveniently on the bureau beside him. He picked it up and stuck it several times into Basil's neck, until at last the man stopped begging Dorian to join him in prayer and repentance.

When he was done, and Basil lay dead, Dorian noticed a new detail in the portrait: blood stained the right hand, the image of the hand with which he had just killed his old friend.

"Cool," he said.

• • •

The next day Dorian blackmailed his friend Alan Campbell into coming over and disposing of the corpse with his fancy chemistry equipment. Fortunately, Alan no sooner finished his work than he went home and hanged himself. Dorian burned every other trace of Basil himself. Then he decided to go smoke some opium.

He took a coach to a distant part of London's waterfront, and went into his favorite old opium den. He had no sooner entered than a woman cried out, "Well, if it ain't Prince Charming!"

Suddenly a sailor who'd been slouched over the bar sat up, just in time to see Dorian hurrying out of the bar. He leaped to his feet, dashed out of the bar, did a cartwheel across the street, caught up to Dorian, slammed him against a wall, and held a gun to his head. It was an impressive burst of energy for a drunk.

"Prince Charming! We meet at last. My name is James Vane. My friends call me Jim. Eighteen years ago, my sister killed herself because of you. You ruined her career, you criticized her makeup, and you broke her heart. Now at last I shall blow your brains out in revenge!"

"Wait!" cried Dorian, "Move into the light . . . look at me . . . do I look like I could have been doing anything besides wetting my diapers eighteen years ago?" James led Dorian out beneath a street lamp, and scrutinized him closely. It was true: such a young, fresh, handsome, sunshiny face could not have been but a toddler so long ago. He apologized and let him go. A woman stepped out of the shadows and cackled, "That was Dorian Gray. He ruined me, too. He hasn't aged a day in eighteen years!"

James Vane, whose friends called him Jim, searched desperately, but Dorian was gone.

• • •

A few days later, while dining with Lord Henry and some other deliciously wicked friends out at his country estate, Dorian suddenly thought he saw James Vane peering in through a window. He passed out from shock, then kept to bed, alone, for three days. Finally he got the better of his fears, and went out one morning to hunt with Lord Filofax and some of the other scathing wits. Suddenly a little fuzzy bunny bounded out of some hedges, and Lord Filofax leveled his gun.

"No!" cried Dorian, who adored little fuzzy bunnies. But it was too late: Lord Filofax had fired. The bullet missed the little fuzzy bunny by twenty yards, but a sudden howl of mortal anguish from the shrubbery suggested the bullet had found a human home. "I believe I've shot one of the beaters," Lord Filofax quipped.

"We'll have to postpone the hunt," Dorian sighed. "Pity."

Later that night a servant came to Dorian's room. Dorian had been expecting the visit.

"Give me the bad news," he said. "How much must I pay his dreadful family?"

The servant shrugged. "I don't know, sir, he ain't one of ours. He was a sailor. He was carrying a gun. He had a big tattoo saying, 'Prince Charming Must Die!' "

Dorian smiled. The next day he returned to town with a light heart.

Several months later, Dorian met Lord Henry for lunch.

"Now, you must tell me where you've been the past few weeks," Lord Henry said. "I hope you were terribly scandalous and that you committed unspeakable acts of depravity. I must know every detail."

Dorian brightened at the opportunity to tell him.

"I did a wonderful thing!" he cried. "I just got back this

morning from a little village where I'd been spending a great deal of time wooing a sweet young creature whom I suddenly chose not to spoil. I left her as innocent as I met her! I'm going to be good, Harry, I truly am, I'm reforming myself!"

"How dull," said Lord Henry, rising from his chair. "The only thing duller than reforming oneself is . . . Well, God, Dorian. You've hit rock bottom."

Dorian ignored his friend's rebuke. He rushed home, eager to see if the picture had registered his kindness, had perhaps become a little less cruel or grotesque as a result of his not having ruined a young woman's life.

But it was only worse! There was more blood on the hands, and the lips were curled more cruelly than ever. Suddenly he realized it had all been vanity. He hadn't spared the girl to do her any kindness; he'd done it because he thought it would be amusing to try something different for a change. In a fit of anger, he seized the knife with which he had killed Basil not so long ago, the knife which he had left here in the secret hidden portrait room even though he'd taken such pains to dispose of all the other evidence, and, holding the knife aloft and screaming wildly, he rushed at the painting.

The butler was the first into the room. It was dusty and full of cobwebs. On the wall hung a lovely portrait of his master, a portrait that captured every golden curl of every golden hair, every glimmer of light that reflected from his sparkling blue eyes, and every fabulous curve of his sumptuous ears. On the floor before the painting lay a hideous and deformed old man, with a knife in his heart.

"Cool," said the butler.

—The End—

Dracula

by Bram Stoker

(1897)

My revenge is just begun! I spread it over centuries, and time is on my side. Your girls that you all love are mine already; and through them you and others shall yet be mine—my creatures, to do my bidding and to be my jackals when I want to feed. Bah!

By the turn of the century, the nations of Western Civilization had woven themselves into a tight and complicated knot of treaties designed to prevent the kind of widespread military conflagration that had plagued Europe at regular intervals since the French Revolution. Sadly, these were weak treaties, many of them having been written on the backs of cocktail napkins or matchbook covers, and pretty much everyone knew that sooner or later it was all going to blow up in their faces. This resulted in repression (see Wilde), alienation (see Kafka), and anxiety (see a psychiatrist). The time was once again ripe for Big Scary Monsters.

Bram Stoker was fifty when he wrote his first novel. Having worked most of his life in theater, he had had ample opportunity to observe beautiful foreigners sustaining themselves on human flesh, and these observations clearly found their way into his work.

Scholars have debated the allegorical meaning of Dracula *from the day it was first published. Scholars who suggest that* Dracula *represents a subliminal rejection of Victorian values, however, have obviously never had sex themselves, and therefore see sex everywhere they look. They should get out more.*

From the Diary of Jonathan Harker

I spent three nights in Budapest awaiting the coach that was to bring me here. Whenever I told the kind and addle-minded peasants of that picturesque backwater where I was headed, the adorable simpletons would cross themselves and kiss their crucifixes. (Crucifices? Crucifi? Note to self: have Mina look it up.) When I finally did get a coach, it stopped at a relay station in a small town near the Transylvanian border. As I waited for the relay there were more amusing peasants, more crossings, more kissings of crucifixes, and one marvelously sincere woman actually hung her crucifix around my neck. I tried to explain that I was from an advanced society in which one no longer worshipped idols, but I could not make myself understood by the simple creature. Everything on this side of the Danube is strange: crossing it from west to east is like crossing from modern civilization into somewhere not as modern or civilized.

At length the relay arrived, and we were on our way. There were more peasants in the coach, staring at me with the same quaint expressions of pity. How I admired their capacity for transforming what must have been profound envy into simple pity!

In the middle of the night the coach came to a stop in the middle of a deep ravine between two high and craggy peaks. Mist filled the air, and the howl of wolves reverberated through the night. A dark gig appeared noiselessly out of nowhere and pulled alongside us. This was the ride the Count had promised to send for me. I transferred myself, happy to take leave of the superstitious peasants and eager to be on the last leg of my journey to a more cosmopolitan companion.

As we made our way to the Count's castle, we passed numerous strange glowing figures in the woods, and several times were surrounded by wolves, to whom the driver spoke sternly, with the air of, oh, say, a supernatural lord issuing commands to his ghastly minions.

Eventually we made it to the castle. The driver let himself in and told me to wait in the coach. Seconds later Count Dracula himself stepped out of the great portico. He looked exactly like the driver, but couldn't have been the same man because the driver had been wearing thick-rimmed black spectacles, and had a bulbous, fleshy nose and a bushy mustache, whereas the Count did not.

The Count told me I must be tired and showed me to my room, where I have been writing these notes. He seems every bit a gentleman. He is very handsome, despite the fact that he has the waxen pallor of a corpse. I've noticed his image is not reflected in mirrors, that his canine teeth are sharpened to fine points, and that his eyes sometimes glow an otherworldly red, but I have been in real estate long enough not to be put off by such things.

Letter from Miss Wilhelmina (Mina) Murray to Miss Lucy Westenra

Dearest Lucy,

I do miss Jonathan ever so much. My only consolation is knowing that once he returns from this business trip we will be married at last. It is my single greatest hope that I shall somehow find a way to be a worthy wife, and that I may be an Englishwoman worthy of such an Englishman, and that we may live in a lovely English house in the lovely English country, and that I may bear him fine English children who will attend fine English schools and eat lovely English muffins, and that the sun shall never set upon the British Empire. Alas, my thoughts turn to him even now, I grow distracted, I can write no more, I must pace and wring my hands and have fainting spells.

How are you?

Full of tender affection and sublimated yearnings, I remain,

Your Mina

Letter from Miss Lucy Westenra to Miss Mina Murray

My Dearest Darling Mina,

I am so sorry you miss Jonathan. His absence must pain you so; truly, a woman is nothing without a man to fill her life. How well you know the emptiness in which my own days have been spent waiting for a man to make me whole. And at last, Mina, at last, today . . . I have been proposed to by two men! Yes, two! Three if you count the American. What is a woman to do? I should have liked to take all three (though I don't mean that in any vulgar way, for well you know my purity and chastity, and that I seek only to find a good

Englishman to whom I can submit completely). The men are Dr.
John Seward, psychiatrist, nice house, good living, even temper, access
to opium; Quincey P. Morris, oil millionaire from Texas, wealthy,
handsome—but American; and Arthur Holmwood, unemployed,
unexceptional, son of a Lord who is expected soon to die. I need not
tell you whom I chose, my friend, for well you know how long my
sympathies have been with the nobility and the glorious institution
of primogeniture! And so I am engaged to be married at last!

Love, kisses, tender caresses, gentle nuzzling,
Your Lucy

From the Diary of Dr. Seward

Patient Renfeld continues to exhibit a strange religious
mania. He continues to talk about the coming of the Master,
and continues to devour insects. Diagnosis: batshit crazy.
Treatment: morphine.

Ms. Lucy Westenra has declined my hand—and, indeed,
all my other parts—in favor of my good friend Arthur
Holmwood. I can hardly blame her: Arthur's virtues are
legion, his character is spotless, his horses are top drawer, and
when his old man dies he gets the whole shebang. Indeed, I
ought to have proposed to him instead of her. Perhaps it's not
too late.

From the Diary of Jonathan Harker

I have made some interesting observations this week.

Early one morning, just before sunrise, I happened to have
crept out of bed and tiptoed around the castle. I accidentally
peeped through a chink in a wall and saw the Count handing
over a bulky burlap sack to three extraordinarily beautiful
women. Their beauty was spellbinding, and their immodest
dress accentuated their wanton curves. Whatever was inside
the bag appeared to be wriggling, and emanated a muffled
wailing sound like that of a newborn child. The women
snatched the bag greedily, licking their lips lasciviously, then

gleefully disappeared with it into thin air. It seemed an odd way to treat an infant. Perhaps they were Hungarian *au pairs;* I must be charitable enough to remember that not everyone has the advantage of English nannies.

Another night I arrived early for dinner and inadvertently peeped through yet another chink in yet another wall—shameful masonry, what?—and I beheld the Count himself laying out my meal. Three *au pairs* to care for a single infant, and a Count who sets his own table! Barbarians!

The Count never dines with me. Whenever I ask why he won't join me, he replies that he's already eaten. He's often got bits of blood around his mouth, so perhaps he's ashamed of his primitive eating habits. Furthermore, the Count seems to sleep all day and go about his business at night. I have tried to explain that when he moves to the new house in England, the purchase of which I am here to help him arrange, he may have to rearrange his schedule, as Englishmen are civilized and will not conduct respectable business after sundown.

The Count made me write several postdated letters addressed to Mina and the firm, explaining in the first that I was finally concluding my business here, in the second that I was in Budapest and on my way back home, and in the third that I had become sick in transit and would probably die. It was difficult writing them, for he forced me to use his pen, which was of course not a fine English pen, but an inferior foreign product.

All the doors to the castle are locked. The only windows I have found open out onto a sheer precipice that drops several thousand feet to the forest below. What a stupid place to have built a castle! No wonder he wants to move to England. Now that I've seen this dreary, ill-conceived place I don't feel so bad selling him a house next door to a lunatic asylum.

One evening while the Count was out I accidentally broke through a locked door—shoddy foreign locksmiths, what?—and passed into a strange room containing only a coffin that bore the inscription, "Dracula." It was a magnificent coffin, framed in dark mahogany and set with precious gems and jewels. As I wondered what sort of morbid vanity could have inspired the Count to have purchased such an object, suddenly those three buxom *au pairs* appeared around me out of thin air and rather begged to kiss me. They grabbed at me, caressed me, tore at my clothes, ran their warm, moist tongues up and down my body, smacking their lips and begging to eat me. Unfortunately the Count appeared and made them go away. He sent me to my room and locked the door. I thought his jealousy most unbecoming.

Lastly, I have observed that every night a little after sundown the Count turns into a bat and flies out his own window. I shouldn't like to think our nobles back home could be so vulgar. Imagine Lord Salisbury flapping about like that! Revolting! Sometimes the Count will take the form of a dog. I should say this was a somewhat more respectable form than a bat, although at least in his bat form he doesn't hump my leg.

These are only some of the many mysteries I have observed and encountered. I begin to suspect something improper is afoot. (Note to self: find a way to get out of here.)

From the Grocery List of Eleanor Simms

Eggs
Bread
Kippers & herring
Chicken
Potatoes & vegetables

From the Diary of Dr. Seward

Patient Renfeld has stopped eating bugs for the time being, although he still speaks of a Master. Religious mania increasing: patient enters an almost rapturous frenzy and shouts, "He is coming! He is on his way!" Diagnosis: batshit crazy. Treatment: morphine.

Letter from Miss Mina Murray to Miss Lucy Westenra

Dearest Lucy,

My worries are over at last! I have received a letter from my beloved Jonathan. He is in Budapest, and will be back on our lovely English soil within a fortnight. I'm a little disappointed in the letter itself—he never once spoke of our wedding, which I have already had to postpone several times on account of his extended absence, but I am so glad to hear from him again that I am willing to overlook everything. At last my Jonathan shall return, and we shall be wed, and I shall be completely actualized as a woman!

Have you married that guy yet, or what?

Kisses, embraces, and tender touches, I remain your loving friend,
Mina

Letter from Arthur Holmwood to Dr. John Seward

Friend John,

I regret I shall be unable to attend the hunting excursion we had planned for Wednesday next, firstly because my father has taken ill and will hopefully soon die, and secondly because, having snatched away the only woman you ever loved, prudence suggests I ought not accompany you into the woods whilst you are carrying a shotgun.

Altogether sincerely,
Arthur

P.S. I have of course assumed your proposal of marriage to have been in jest.

Telegram from Miss Lucy Westenra to Miss Mina Murray

Terrible news: Arthur's father still alive. Will come visit you at seashore by next train. Arthur staying behind to do what he can.
L.

From the Diary of Miss Mina Murray

Still no further word from Jonathan. I worry. Lucy has been here at the house in Whitby with me almost two weeks now. We take long walks together along the harbor and sit on a little stone bench by the lighthouse and tell each other sweet tales of how fine and English our lives will be when we're finally married to the fine respectable Englishmen we love. There's a graveyard there and it's quite peaceful, as the dead tend to be quiet.

Lucy has been sleepwalking at night, which I find odd. I think her future father-in-law's stubborn clinging to life is beginning to wear on her. It really would be better for everyone if he would just knock off and be done with it—these old lords can be so selfish!

Excerpt from an Article in the Whitby *Dailygraph*

Lord & Lady Preswick of Warwick Lane are pleased to report the engagement of their disagreeable daughter Eleanor to Mr. Eugene Weldon Spitshire, unpleasant son of Colonel Albert and Mrs. Penelope Spitshire of Harkwood. The objectionable couple will be wed next spring. . . .

Excerpt from *Another* Article in the Whitby *Dailygraph*

No inhabitant or summer visitor need be told of the fierce winds, driving rain, pounding surf, or mysterious fog that set upon our pleasant seaside community so suddenly yesterday, nor need they be told how a mysterious ship, flying flags from a godforsaken eastern European principality, stole its way into the harbor at the height of this storm, nor how the brave men and women who rushed to the aid of the beached ship discovered only one man on board—nor how that man was in fact a corpse tied fast to the wheel, nor how in his death grip he clutched a rosary, nor how his journal revealed that the ship had been carrying a mysterious cargo that frightened all the crew, nor how the crew had apparently disappeared over the course of the voyage, man by man, in some strange way related to that awful box in the ship's hold, nor how the only sign of life on board was a fierce dog that leaped off the ship as soon as she had struck land, nor how said canine bounded off into the woods never more to be seen. Indeed, every particular of these extraordinary circumstances is so well known to every man, woman, and child in Whitby that any further narrative by this reporter would be superfluous.

From the Diary of Dr. Seward

Patient Renfeld grew calm yesterday, and spoke lucidly and at length about the societal impact of heavy industry on agrarian economies and the possible political and economic applications of the Hegelian dialectic, until suddenly freezing up at one point, glancing out the window, and muttering merely: "He is come!" He has not spoken since. Diagnosis: batshit crazy. Treatment: morphine.

From the Diary of Miss Mina Murray

Things have taken rather an interesting turn. I awoke last night to find that Lucy was no longer beside me in bed, and had apparently slipped out the window in one of her sleepwalking episodes. Without even changing out of my scanty nightdress, which clung to my every sensuous curve, I rushed out of the house and straight to the only place I could have imagined her going: our stone bench by the cemetery at the top of the hill overlooking the harbor. Indeed, once I had rushed through the little town square to the foot of the hill, I caught sight of her immediately. There she sat on the bench, but there appeared to be a man behind her: a dark, cloaked figure with glowing red eyes. Ignoring my own safety, I called out at once, and I saw those searing red eyes glance down at me. Undaunted, plucking up my fine English courage, I rushed straight up the hill. I could not keep my eyes upon them as I ran, however, and by the time I reached the bench the gentleman with the red eyes was gone.

I brought Lucy back to bed without waking her, for she was still in a somnambulant state, but when I put her to bed I noticed two puncture marks in her throat, each of them dribbling a little bit of blood. Doubtless the stranger had been a benevolent doctor trying to treat her sleepwalking with a bleeding cure. She slept quite soundly all night, and indeed, though it is late in the morning she sleeps still. She must be really tired.

I should have liked to write more, but I have just received a note from my darling Jonathan: he is returned to England, but is in hospital at Stratfordshiretonville. His letter was forwarded by a nurse who says he is recovering from a terrible trauma. His body is covered with welts and bruises, he is wildly disoriented, he sobs in his sleep, and both his ears are broken. It is the doctor's diagnosis that Jonathan's trauma may have been caused by his having crawled from Hungary to France, then having swum from Calais to the lovely White Cliffs of Dover, all to evade some mysterious and powerful stranger. My poor darling! I must go at once!

From the Diary of Dr. Seward

Received a note from Miss Mina Murray this morning, asking that I look in on a friend whom circumstances have compelled her to leave temporarily, but whom she felt could benefit from the visit of a doctor. Imagine my astonishment to discover that this "friend" was my dear Lucy, the very woman I had hoped to make my wife!

Lucy had apparently been sleeping some fourteen hours by the time I made my visit. Miss Murray was on her way north to visit her fiancé, a Mr. Jonathan Harker, and wanted to be sure that Lucy would be cared for in her absence. Lucy's mother is staying at the same house, of course, but her heart is weak and it is feared that concern for her daughter could kill her dead. Miss Murray and I therefore told her that everything was fine, there was nothing to worry about, and that there would be no need for her to look in upon her daughter for several days, as it was absolutely improbable that Lucy would die that quickly.

I examined Lucy carefully, slowly and carefully, and rather appreciatively. I found nothing out of the ordinary besides two puncture marks in her neck. Mina assured me these were the work of a benevolent wandering red-eyed doctor who had tried bleeding Lucy out of sleepwalking, but I am not so sure. Present diagnosis: measles. But I have sent for my old professor to rule out the one possibility too terrible to contemplate.

Telegram from Abraham Van Helsing, MD, PhD, Y2K, etc., etc., to Dr. Seward

Friend John. Receiving your telegram I am. Much concern also sharing I am. Come I at once will. So much the haste make I that spin will your head! Happy again at seeing with old student favorite of mine. Yours in celery, Van Helsing.

Letter from Arthur Holmwood to Miss Lucy Westenra

Good news, my darling! Father has lost consciousness and is expected soon to die. I shall be Lord Goddammitall before the week is out.

I hear you are ill. That is disagreeable, darling. I should quite appreciate your not being ill upon my return.

Rather sincerely,

Hon. Arthur Holmwood

From Mina Harker's Diary

This morning I awoke not as Miss Mina Murray, but as Mrs. Jonathan Harker! At last I feel a sense of identity!

We were wed hastily here at the country estate of Jonathan's employer, Mr. Hawkins, who bid us marry quickly so that he could leave his millions and his estate to us upon his death, which is expected momentarily—ah! that must have been it just now.

So Jonathan and I are married at last, are wealthy beyond our wildest expectations, and yet all is not roses. While Jonathan was recovering I inadvertently read the diary of his trip to the Count's castle. What I read chills my bones to the marrow. Clearly Count Dracula is some manner of monster, and he is now loose upon our fine English soil. It cannot be allowed! And I wonder more now about those twin punctures on Lucy's tender neck . . . about the dog that bounded off the foreign ship . . . about the unusual new tenant Dr. Seward mentioned having moved in to the house next door to his asylum. I begin to feel that dreadful things are afoot, that we have all become entangled in some terrible gothic horror story from which we shall not escape alive.

From the Journal of Abraham Van Helsing, MD, PhD, Y2K, etc., etc.

Never mind about experiment with Swedish twins! . . . In London am arrived for quite curious case suggesting to me of vampires. Patient is Miss Lucy, very lovely girl, with the bosom full and heaving, but has been several times to be bitten by the vampire. Very weak, very feeble, so have given three transfusion of the blood. One from fiancé, Lord Goddammitall, whose father is just recently dead and who are therefore arrived only few days ago. One from rejected fiancé American by name of Quincey P. Morris. One from rejected fiancé of hers and student former favorite of mine, Jack Seward. All the transfusion somehow sucked out every night despite how careful we are to be watching her! So much the confusion! Much love and devotion for Miss Lucy!

We watching her, watching her. (But sometime we go for sandwich.) Last night she is sucked to death anyway. Her mother find her there dead in morning and so very upset is she, good mother of Miss Lucy, that she also die, too. Very sad is everyone, but know do I that if Miss Lucy bitten truly by vampire, we not have seen last of her. We wait for her tonight at grave, and if we see her—ha! We chop off head and drive stake through heart. How I love to chop off head and drive stake through heart! It give me only pleasure of job. But alas, there so many head and heart, and so little of the time. . . .

From Lord Goddammitall's Valet's Notebook

His lordship out all night last night. Items to be laundered: one overcoat, blood-soaked. One pair gloves, blood-soaked. One blue suit, Harrods, blood-soaked. One white shirt, Harrods, blood-soaked. One paisley pattern ascot, of French manufacture, blood-soaked. One pair leather shoes, of Italian manufacture, caked in mud and dried blood. His lordship reports that source of blood was fox from last night's midnight hunting expedition with Messieurs Seward, Morris, Harker, and Van Helsing. Have recommended his lordship hunt with better shots in future. Or hunt in daylight.

From Jonathan Harker's Diary

Earlier this week we took care of Lucy, and only the knowledge that we have saved her soul from eternal damnation mitigates the terrible memory of watching Lord Goddammitall and Dr. Van Helsing pound a stake through her heart and chop off her head in the crypt.

I fear that Mina has become the Count's next victim: she exhibits all the same symptoms Lucy did. Dr. Van Helsing says that if we can find all the dirt the Count shipped to London and bless it with communion wafers, then the Count will have nowhere safe to live and will die. Our investigations have revealed the Count brought thirty boxes of dirt into England (as if we hadn't quite more than enough already!), and we have already done away with most of them. This afternoon we will break into his house in the city and take care of the last of his dirt, and this whole sordid business will be behind us.

From Dr. Seward's Diary

We broke into the Count's pied-à-terre not long before sunset. We found all the remaining boxes of dirt, and Dr. Van Helsing purified them all. We were quite satisfied: there was no longer any safe haven for the foul fiend on our blessed isle!

Just as we were preparing to leave, however, we heard steps coming up the front stairs, and then a key turning in the lock. We froze and looked at one another in terror: Dr. Van Helsing, Lord Goddammitall, Jonathan, Quincey, and myself were all reduced to statues in our fear. Not literally, of course: I mean to say only that we became as immobile as statues—specifically, statues of marble or granite that do not move.

The Count entered the room and, in a single supernatural leap, was upon Jonathan. We all pulled out our crucifixes and held them before the demon, and he cowered back against a wall.

"Now," said Dr. Van Helsing, unfortunately the first of us to regain the faculty of speech. "Now, Count Dracula, your dirt polluted all is with the holy wafer, and as no place left is there in England for you, you shall die, not die like already dead you are, but die again, like die the people normal, who not becoming vampires are, and rid of you shall be the world!"

The Count's eyes glowed fierce like coals—coals that have been set on fire some time ago and have burned well through—and he groped his way along the wall toward a window.

"Why you are not so bold as late have you been, Herr Count? Why you slide the wall along as though in hope to be escaped from this doom certain? No escape is there for you, monster of the night, sucker of the blood, wastrel of the ladies! Perish must you now!"

"Ha!" roared the Count. "I am not a man, I am a force of nature. You will no sooner stop me than you will stop any other force of nature, such as a hurricane, for example. You are too late! I have already tasted the women you love, and they are mine. My work here is done. I will return to my homeland for now, but I shall return!"

With that he leaped out through a window onto the street, and disappeared into the crowd. We split up and ran after him in every direction, but could not find him. Dr. Van Helsing says that surely he back to Transylvania a way must have found, travel must he by boat—conveniently enough, it appears that vampires can only travel by boat when they're being chased by three Englishmen, an American, and a foreigner with an indeterminate but comical accent.

P.S. Found patient Renfeld dead in his room the other day, strangled to death, his head nearly ripped off his shoulders. Diagnosis: suicide.

From Mina Harker's Diary

[*Two months later*]

I have been so busy lately, there simply hasn't been time to keep up. Anyway, lots has happened, it was every exciting, everyone's fine—except of course Count Dracula and those horrid Hungarian *au pairs,* who are altogether done with—and one of these days I'll have to tell you all about it.

M.

—The End—

Legal note: *While vampirism is a popular superstition dating waaaaaay back, stabbing someone through the heart and chopping their head off is still not considered justifiable homicide by any judicial system outside Los Angeles.*

The Metamorphosis

by Franz Kafka

(1915)

They were now mostly very silent. Soon after supper his father would fall asleep in his armchair; his mother and sister would admonish each other to be silent; his mother, bending low over the lamp, stitched at fine sewing for an underwear firm; his sister, who had taken a job as a salesgirl, was learning shorthand and French in the evenings on the chance of bettering herself. Sometimes his father woke up and as if quite unaware that he had been sleeping said to his mother: "What a lot of sewing you're doing today!" and at once fell asleep again, while the two women exchanged a tired smile.

In the summer of 1914, Austrian Archduke Franz Ferdinand was assassinated in Sarajevo. As a result, Austria declared war on Serbia, Russia declared war on Austria, Germany declared war on Russia, France declared war on Germany, Germany declared war on England, and England became indignant. By the end of summer, all of the Great Powers and most of the Very Good Powers of Europe had picked sides and started shooting at one another. The Industrial Revolution had improved man's ability to blow the living shit out of his fellow creature, however, and the ease with which the elegance and gentility of the old world were blasted into oblivion shocked and horrified everyone to the extent that it seemed only logical that people should turn into insects. Franz Kafka therefore wrote The Metamorphosis.

*Franz Kafka's novels and novellas are so Kafkaesque that one has to wonder at the enormity of coincidence required to have produced a writer named Kafka to write them. A bourgeois Czech insurance underling, Kafka was gifted with a boundless imagination and an acute case of paranoia, both of which found an outlet in his writings. Despite the tremendous success and popularity of his work, many of the novels of which he was proudest never saw publication (*Someone's Trying to Kill Me, They're Watching Me, Watching Me!, *and* For God's Sake, Don't Look, Just Pretend They're Not There*). Kafka never married, but he did have a series of Czech mates. At the peak of his writing, Kafka became "sick" and "died."*

As Gregor Samsa awoke one morning from uneasy dreams he found himself transformed in his bed into a gigantic insect. He lay on his hard, armored back and looked down upon the sectioned arches of his belly, and at the many absurd little legs, so frail in comparison to the rest of his body, quivering helplessly.

How odd, he thought: I must have overslept.

He tried to swing his legs down off the bed and get up, at which point a resistance from his lower body reminded him that he no longer had two long legs extending from his waist, but rather dozens of little twitchy ones sticking up from his belly.

Well, he thought, goddamn.

And again he tried to move himself out of bed, and again nothing happened. He looked down at his body and wondered how it was that he had become an insect. He hadn't been an insect when he'd gone to sleep. He hadn't been an insect on the train back from Dankelschnitzenberg. He hadn't been an insect on any of the sales calls he'd made on that trip—not technically. Not literally. It was true that circumstances had required him to become a sort of slave to the commercial-industrial complex, and that in serving these modern demigods, that had reduced so much of humanity to mere ciphers, he had sometimes abased himself to the level of an insect, but so had lots of other people and none of them were bugs. How was he supposed to get to the office like this? How could he meet with clients? How could a big bug charm them into buying his firm's own brand of soul-deadening commercialism? It was all a big pain in the ass.

He heard a knock at his door, then his mother's voice. "Gregor, are you still here? Haven't you a train to catch? Is everything all right?"

Gregor was glad his many years of travelling for the firm had gotten him into the habit of always locking his door, even at home—especially at home. "I'm not feeling well," he said.

"You don't sound well," his mother said, and she was right: his voice had an unnaturally twittering screech. "Perhaps you've got that bug that's been going around." She didn't realize the irony of what she'd said, of course, for she was estranged and alienated from the truth of the dread engines driving the dehumanizing culture of the society in which she lived.

Gregor focused very hard and spoke very slowly. "I'm up," he said, "I'll be out of bed soon." It was difficult to make his voice come out the way he wanted it to, in much the same way that the constricting forces of social repression made it difficult for one to be an individual.

Gregor struggled to get out of the bed, casting his weight this way and that in an attempt to flip himself out, since those shivering little legs were obviously of no use. He could hear his family fretting about him out in the hallway, and even heard his sister, Grete, sobbing at one point. He was relieved when he heard his mother send her for the doctor, because he'd begun to fear Grete would try to force herself into his room some way or other, and though he wasn't sure which parts of him were which, there was certainly no question but that he was entirely naked. He was ashamed of his nakedness despite the fact that nudity was of course a perfectly natural state in which no one ought to feel the slightest shame, least of all a bug without any recognizable genitals.

At last Gregor managed to rock himself out of the bed, and he crashed to the floor with a terrible thud that shook the very walls of his little room. He landed on his feet, and as useless as they may have been when he lay prostrate, they certainly knew what they were about now. Yes, he was certainly an insect, but he was a mobile little bugger, and he couldn't see any reason why he couldn't put on a suit and make his way to the office.

As he picked his way through his drawers and closet looking for something that might fit him in his present condition—wondering, for example, which necktie might set his hard brown face, fuzzy black mandibles, bulging black orbs, and slender antennae to their best advantage—there came a knock at his door.

"Gregor," he heard his father say, "Gregor, the chief clerk's here." He heard his father making pathetic bourgeois apologies to the chief clerk, and could actually hear the chief clerk sighing as though he'd heard it all before.

Gregor didn't like the chief clerk. Gregor didn't like any of the clerks. As a matter of fact, Gregor didn't like much of anyone but his sister. He was going to pay her tuition for the conservatory as a Christmas present this year. Wouldn't she be grateful? He imagined the look on her face when he told her. He'd tell her privately, by the fire, whispering so she'd have to bring her fresh, young, lovely face near his to hear it, and the glow of the fire would spread rosy light across her cheeks. . . .

"Gregor, the old man is wondering about you. We've all been wondering about you. You're rather late, you know." The chief clerk was a soulless bureaucrat who had sacrificed his own humanity on the altar of commercial enterprise. Gregor didn't like him, because Gregor still had some humanity left in him, even though he was now himself a cockroach.

"For God's sake," Gregor cried, "I'm sick! Can't a man be sick now and then?"

There was silence from the other side of the door, followed by low murmurs.

"Can't I be sick now and then?" Gregor repeated.

"Listen," came the imperious reply of the chief clerk (who had, it should be known, kicked several small dogs on the way to the Samsa household), "listen, you've got it nice and posh travelling around the way you do, Gregor, but the other clerks and I toil away in the office for twelve or fourteen hours a day, seven days a week, thirty-one days a month, except for those months such as September, which have only thirty days, and of course February, which may have twenty-eight or twenty-nine, as the case may be—but, Gregor, we realize that the wheels of industry stop for no man, and as we treasure our jobs and our salaries, so we suffer through our little ailments and do our work each day without complaint. I will tell you something, Gregor: there has been talk in the office. Indeed, there is often talk in the office, as we have business to conduct which sometimes requires talking, but the particular kind of talking to which I'm alluding is that of a rather malicious nature, if you follow me. Do you follow me, Gregor? Do you? And I don't just ask metaphorically, although I assure you the metaphor is apt, but I ask also rather literally, since as I speak I am gathering my scarf about me, pulling my hat down tight over my head, and preparing to leave, and I cannot too strongly state my preference, for your own welfare, and that of the family which you support by means of this profession, and to which profession you are shackled by an advance of cash our master lent your family some years ago when things were not so rosy on account of your father's business having gone bankrupt—in a lovely metaphor for the moral condition of our times—all of those parenthetical observations notwithstanding, Gregor, I cannot state too strongly my preference that you follow me back to that office and resume your duties at once."

While the chief clerk had been rambling along so parenthetically, Gregor had managed to accomplish two things: he had pulled himself upright alongside the door, and he had placed one of his twitchy little feet upon the key. Now he turned the key and pulled the door open, leaned himself against the jamb, and smiled out at the chief clerk.

"I'll come in to the office," Gregor said coolly, "but I'm damned if I'm wearing trousers."

The chief clerk retreated hastily while Gregor's parents stared at him in horror. At last his mother fainted completely away, as any good turn-of-the-century mother would, and his father kicked him back into his room, locking it from the outside.

Gregor crawled under his bed, a position which he found inexplicably comfortable, and tried to decide what to do next. Here he was, twenty-nine years old, without a job, without a wife, without the sympathy of his family, and without a good pile of steaming dung to crawl around in.

I wonder what I shall do, he wondered, and he began pacing his room as was his habit when thinking. He paced up and down the little room, but he soon found he had to crawl about on the walls and ceiling if he really wanted to do any good pacing.

He crawled about for hours, stopping only now and then to concentrate his attention on any conversations taking place outside his room. He learned that his family had somehow gotten rid of the doctor whom Grete had brought back with her, and that Grete had come to know of his condition. He discerned that his whole family was distraught, and that the servants were suspicious. He learned that Hans Klapper down on Cheeseburgerstrasse had raised the price of his strudel again, that Maria Hotten-Trotten was carrying a French earl's child, and that those awful Bulow boys were up to no good. It was all very dreary, very bourgeois, and very alienating. At last he found himself hanging lethargically from the ceiling, lost in his own sad and terrible and bourgeois thoughts, and gradually he fell asleep.

The days and weeks that followed were bleak and terrible. Though his family seemed to have accepted his condition, and though Grete was careful to bring in water and bits of garbage for him to eat, he knew they found the situation intolerable. He wasn't any too pleased with things himself. The servants gradually fled, all of them being replaced by one bold maid who seemed oddly indifferent to Gregor's condition, probably because her proletarian sensibilities made her purer and more humane. His father had to begin working again, his sister was looking for employment, and his mother was reduced to doing all the chores formerly done by the servants in addition to getting a job of her own as a seamstress. Things eventually became so difficult that they had to take in boarders to make ends meet. Three big gentlemen moved into Grete's room, forcing Grete to move into the broom closet, in much the same way that industry and commerce were shepherding people into lives of dreary utility.

Gregor just crawled about his room each day, reflecting on the strange turn of events and getting depressed and not eating much. This state of affairs lasted for months, until one evening things finally came to a head.

The boarders had come home a little drunk, and demanded that Grete play the violin for them. The family and the boarders gathered around a roaring fire in the living room, and Grete began to play.

Gregor heard the music from his room, and it put him into a strange kind of trance. The music captivated him, it called out to him, it seemed to communicate the very essence of his sister's sweetness. It was not the quality of the music that enchanted him—for there was none—but the delicate and mournful way his sister scratched at the bowstrings. He was drawn inexorably to her. Fortunately the maid had sensed that the story was almost over, so she had left Gregor's room unlocked and he was able to creep into the living room unnoticed.

But he could not hold himself back from the music, could not keep himself from crawling toward his sister. Onward he crept, oblivious to everything but Grete.

The largest of the three boarders suddenly rose, his face reddening, his fists clenching, his eyes riveted upon Gregor's creeping form.

Gregor's father noticed the man's discomfort at once. "Would you like a laxative?" he asked bourgeoisly.

"There is a giant cockroach there in the hallway," said the boarder. "That is bad enough. Coupled with your daughter's grotesque abuse of this fine instrument, it is all too much to take. The emperor ought to pass a proclamation making it unlawful *on pain of death* for your daughter ever again to look at a violin, much less play one. Come along, gentlemen."

And all three boarders abruptly left.

Gregor's father turned furiously upon his son. "Look what you've done, you damned insect! Good boarders, good money, and you've scared them off for good! You'll make a scandal! Grete will never find a husband! We'll have to move to a cramped apartment and eat horrid food that our poverty will force us to cook ourselves. You filthy bug! I'll kill you, kill you!"

Gregor turned his head wearily to Grete. Surely she would understand. But she was already removing a shoe from one foot. "Get him with this, father—squash him! Kill him!"

His mother only sobbed. The betrayal was complete: their bourgeois prejudices had finally succeeded in overcoming whatever little family feeling had let them tolerate Gregor this long. Gregor could bear his sorrow no longer. With a heavy heart he crawled back into his room and died.

Later the maid, that good peasant woman who was not caught in the tangle of alienating bourgeois prejudices that had corrupted the whole Samsa family, came in and dragged the dead bug to the toilet, where she flushed him to oblivion.

Gregor's parents made out very nicely in their new jobs, and Grete made a good marriage less than a year later, because they were foolish bourgeois conformists and had only loved their son and brother so long as he conformed to their narrow, petty worldview.

—The End—

Historical postscript: *Anyone who wasn't killed or maimed by the Great War was dehumanized or alienated, or at least made very nervous. Kafka had clearly seen it coming all along, well before the "illness" that led to his "death." Who silenced him? On what authority? Toward what end?*

We may never know.

Ulysses

by James Joyce

(1922)

... and how he kissed me under the Moorish wall and I thought well as well him as another and then I asked him with my eyes to ask again yes and then he asked me would I yes to say yes my mountain flower and first I put my arms around him yes and drew him down to me so he could feel my breasts all perfume yes and his heart was going like mad and yes I said yes I will Yes.

The confusion of the Great War was so profound that writers around the world had all sense of grammar, syntax, and structure knocked clean out of their heads.

Like so many brilliant Irish writers before and after him, James Joyce was a drunken madman who got the hell out of Ireland as soon as he could afford a passport. Living in Paris among the other drunken expatriates, he wrote a nice little book of stories about the men and women of Dublin, and a promising literary career opened itself up before him. Unfortunately this was in 1914, and the shadow of war threatened to interrupt his incessant revelry and drunken debauches along the Seine. Joyce was strongly antiwar—he was anti anything that interfered with a good debauch—so he fled Paris. Sadly, on his way out of the city he was struck in the head by a flying baguette, and he never wrote nice little stories again.

Ulysses is often cited as the most important literary accomplishment of our age, and as soon as someone translates it we'll know for sure. In fact, Joyce himself bragged about the troubles subsequent generations would have in understanding his work. While Ulysses is not as difficult a novel as Finnegans Wake, this is akin to saying a bullet between the eyes is not as difficult as a half dozen grenades up one's ass. Ulysses was recently selected as the greatest English-language novel ever published, and this was surprising on many levels—not least of them the astonishing revelation that Ulysses was written in English.

June 16 came and went in Dublin.

—The End—

1984

by George Orwell

(1949)

When we are omnipotent we shall have no more need of science. . . . All competing pleasures will be destroyed. . . . If you want a picture of the future, imagine a boot stamping on a human face—forever.

At the time in which 1984 *was written, most of Western Civilization was struggling against the specter of totalitarianism. (This should not be confused with the* scepter *of totalitarianism, which was a little stick that Stalin liked to shake at people.) Totalitarianism was the political theory that the state should have total control over every citizen, with only a few select exceptions—for example, those who had come up with the theory.*

British writer Eric Blair (George Orwell) had developed an alternative theory, namely that the tyrannical subjugation of the masses by means of torture and brainwashing was a bad idea, and he set out to write a book that would illustrate this controversial hypothesis. As such, 1984 *has a place alongside such happy classics as H. G. Wells's* The Time Machine, *Ayn Rand's* Anthem, *Aldous Huxley's* Brave New World, *Eugene Zamyatin's* We, *and Hanna-Barbera's* The Jetsons. *Fortunately, the year 1984 has come and gone without many of Orwell's nightmares coming true, although he did clearly foresee the demonic tyranny of aerobics instructors.*

It was a bright cold day in April, and the clocks were striking thirteen: it was the future, and everything sucked. Winston Smith had been just a boy at the time of the revolutions, but even he knew that somehow things had not always sucked this bad.

He hurried out of the bitter wind into Victory Mansions and upstairs to his apartment. In the hallway he passed a big poster that portrayed the face of a ruggedly handsome man, about forty-five years old, with a dark mustache. It was one of those posters whose eyes were designed in such a way that wherever you went the eyes appeared to be following you. (They used to have those jiggly eyes, that would look all over when you shook them, but those had been fun, and the Party had eventually settled on an iron-clad policy of No Fun.) Below the face were the words BIG BROTHER IS WATCHING YOU. This was also a recent innovation, having ten years ago replaced the original slogan, YOU'RE UNDER CONSTANT SURVEILLANCE, MAGGOT.

Winston let himself into his room. The telescreen was on, of course—it was impossible to turn off—and the announcer was talking in excited tones about the bold new offensive against Eurasia. Winston looked out the window at the dreary London skyline, which had never been rebuilt since the wars of the fifties, and which was now dwarfed by the Party ministries, whose pyramidal architecture rose imposingly above the city: the Ministry of Peace, which dealt with war; the Ministry of Love, which dealt with punishment; the Ministry of Truth, which dealt with propaganda; and the Ministry of Cute Little Puppy Dogs, which dealt with cats. Winston worked in the Ministry of Truth, from which he had just come home on his lunch hour to commit an act of such enormous defiance that it would set an entire novel in motion. Before this quiet but colossal act of rebellion, however, Winston noted the slogans etched into the whitewashed, windowless sides of the mammoth Ministry of Love.

WAR IS PEACE

FREEDOM IS SLAVERY

IGNORANCE IS STRENGTH

BUT DIAMONDS ARE A GIRL'S BEST FRIEND

Hate Week was not far off, Winston remembered, taking care of the last bit of exposition necessary before beginning things in earnest. He stepped into an alcove beside the telescreen, the only part of his cramped and dreary little apartment into which the telescreen could not see, and withdrew from his desk a little cream-colored diary and a blue fountain pen, which he had bought the other day from an illegal diary and fountain pen dealer operating out of a cramped and dreary antique store in one of the prole districts. He began, against all laws and regulations, to write in the book, slowly and carefully at first, then a little wildly, eventually degrading to angry squigglies.

April 4, 1984. I hate the future: everything sucks. Things were better in the old days, when things didn't suck as bad. Some things didn't even suck at all. You know who really pisses me off is that dark-haired woman I'm always bumping into at work. It pisses me off that I can't shag her. She belongs to the Anti-Sex League. The Anti-Sex League sucks. Everything sucks. I hate my job. I think my section chief O'Brien agrees. I saw him looking at me once during the two-minute hate and I thought I saw a look in his eye that said: "Doesn't this suck?" and I looked back at him for just a second with a look that said: "yes i think this sucks," and i'd swear he was looking back at me with a look that said well then we're both agreed that this sucks and so i looked back with a look of yes we certainly do agree on that and even though it was very short it made me feel much better because everything really does suck. . . .

The worst crime of all was thoughtcrime, and he knew he was guilty. It was only a matter of time before he would be caught, taken to the Ministry of Love, executed, and tortured (although probably not in that order). He knew he was a doomed man. "I'm a doomed man," he wrote.

And then: "Doom sucks."

The next morning there were some exciting projects lined up for him on his cubicle desk at the Ministry of Truth, where he spent his days rewriting old newspaper and history book articles to reflect the truth as adjusted by the Party. Little pneumatic tubes would cough up work projects onto his desk, and he would dictate the revised pieces into the speak-write. That was his job. It was very futuristic.

He had lunch with people he didn't like down in the canteen. This was inevitable, because he didn't like anyone. Maybe O'Brien, but O'Brien was Inner Party and therefore never had to eat in the canteen. While they ate, the telescreens in the canteen announced that Oceania's standard of living had risen another twenty percent that afternoon. Everyone applauded. The telescreen announced that another battle had been won against Eurasia, and everyone applauded. The telescreen announced that Big Brother wanted everyone to stand up, and everyone stood up. It announced that Big Brother wanted everyone to sit down, and everyone sat down. It announced that everyone should stand on one leg, and a few people did, and they were taken out and shot because Big Brother hadn't said to.

A few days later at work Winston saw the dark-haired woman walking down a hallway towards him. He tried not to look at her, but he couldn't help it. She was very attractive. She had breasts and legs and everything.

Suddenly she tripped and fell, and he rushed over to help her up. She took his hand, pulled herself up, and walked on without saying anything, not even "thank you." But Winston felt a piece of paper in his hand. There was a telescreen right there, so he couldn't look at it yet, but when he finally did have a moment of privacy later in the day he read it. It said, "I love you."

That didn't suck.

He tried for two weeks to get alone with her, out of earshot of a telescreen, and finally succeeded. They sat together at a lunch table in the canteen, and spoke quietly and without looking at one another while they ate their charred black lumps of food, which sucked.

"Mmmph bllgr glmmph mmpl glmm," she said.

"Don't talk with your mouth full," he said.

She swallowed.

"Take the train to the country and get off at a certain stop and walk to a field and there's some bushes and then there's a tree and behind it there's a grove of more trees and behind that there's a clearing."

"Yes," Winston said, "I've been there before."

"Meet me there at 1830 on Friday night. I may be a little late. Be careful."

"I will," Winston said.

She showed up just a little after him that night, and immediately tore off her clothes. Her body was every bit as magnificent as he'd imagined: she had breasts and legs and everything.

Later he said, "We should do this more often."

"Okay," she said. Then they went back to the city, separately.

It was hard getting out to the country as often as he'd have liked (approximately every forty-five minutes), so Winston made a secret deal with the illegal diary and fountain pen dealer for regular use of the apartment over the antique store. It was an old-fashioned little room with a twelve-hour clock and a four-poster bed and a one-fire stove. Winston and Julia—that was her name, the dark-haired woman with the breasts, etc.—met in this room once or twice a week, as their schedules permitted, and they would have secret sex and lie around and talk about how much everything sucked. They wished they could get married, but Winston was already married to a nasty old skank who'd disappeared years ago, and Julia was a member of the Anti-Sex League.

One day Winston's section chief approached his cubicle. This was O'Brien, the Inner Party man Winston suspected of secretly sharing his view that everything sucked.

"I've been reading your columns," O'Brien said, "and I notice your use of Newspeak is fairly good. You might like to come by my house some time and take a look at the eleventh edition of the Newspeak dictionary. It hasn't appeared in stores yet, of course, but I've got a nice advance copy. Here's my address, come by any time."

O'Brien held his address out in such a way that the tele-screen was sure to see it, which Winston thought awfully clever. The Party would suspect nothing, and yet it was clear O'Brien was inviting Winston to come by his house and talk privately about how much everything sucked. And maybe, just maybe, he'd invite Winston to join the Brotherhood.

He brought Julia with him to O'Brien's one day a few weeks later. It was a great big house in the middle of the fancy Inner Party neighborhood. A servant led Winston and Julia into O'Brien's study. O'Brien dismissed the servant, turned off the telescreen, and asked his guests to sit down.

"You can turn the telescreen off?" Winston asked.

"Certainly. It's one of the Inner Party privileges. And we're allowed to pee standing up."

"Lucky bastards," Julia said.

There was an uncomfortable silence. Winston was suddenly nervous. O'Brien said nothing, gave no indication what he was expecting. Julia said nothing either. Several moments passed, then Winston said nothing again, O'Brien didn't reply, and Julia had nothing to add.

"Why are you here?" O'Brien finally asked.

"Everything sucks," Winston blurted.

"Ah," said O'Brien.

"Everything sucks, so I want to join the Brotherhood and dedicate my life to fighting the Party."

"I see," said O'Brien. "And what about her?"

"I'll do whatever he does," Julia said, "because dammit, that's just the kind of futuristic rebel woman I am."

"I see," said O'Brien. "Very good. Are you willing to die for the Brotherhood?"

"Yes," they answered as one.

"Are you willing to kill for the Brotherhood?"

"Yes," they answered again.

"Would you be willing to commit acts of sabotage, that could result in the deaths of hundreds of innocent people, for the Brotherhood?"

"Yes."

"Would you kill an innocent child for the Brotherhood?"

"Yes."

"Would you splash acid in a baby's face for the Brotherhood?"

"Yes."

"Would you put a little kitten into a blender and hit the 'liquefy' button for the Brotherhood?"

"Yes."

"Even if it was an adorable little kitty-cat?"

"Yes."

"Even if it was looking at you with those big kitty-cat eyes, and going *meow, meow,* and just so cute you could scream?"

"Yes."

"Really? Wow. And would you betray each other?"

"Yes," Winston said.

"No," Julia said.

"No," Winston said.

"I see," O'Brien said. "That's good to know. Now go home and pretend nothing has happened. You'll never know you're part of the Brotherhood, you'll never meet any other members, you'll never know that anything's different at all. Some time when you don't expect it a man will hand you a briefcase, Winston, since you're the man, and in the briefcase will be a copy of *the book,* which explains everything. You may leave now."

So they left.

• • •

Hate Week came at last, and all of London—indeed, all of Oceania—lathered itself into a fine foaming frenzy, chanting hate for Eurasia and all other enemies of Big Brother, gathering in every public street and square to shout their hate, stamp their feet, and pound their fists; and then, suddenly, incomprehensibly, the gathered throngs all began rushing about for hats; there was a mad panic; a terrible rush; everyone everywhere had to have a hat and had to have it at once; there was violence, rioting. Apparently there'd been a typo somewhere, and the telescreens were suddenly telling everyone to celebrate Hat Week. Since the telescreen was run by the Party, and since the Party was never wrong, it was suddenly vitally necessary to celebrate Hat Week. Winston got a nice fedora; Julia found a charming little pillbox. Anyone not wearing a hat was taken out and shot.

In the madness of the crowd, someone came up to Winston and said, "I think you dropped your briefcase."

"I didn't bring my briefcase," Winston shouted back. The crowd was noisy.

"I think you did," the stranger roared.

"I'm pretty sure I didn't," Winston thundered.

"Take the damn briefcase already," Julia said, and suddenly Winston remembered about *the book.*

"Sorry," he said, taking the briefcase.

And the stranger was gone.

A few days later Winston lay in the big four-poster bed of his and Julia's secret love nest. Julia would still be another hour; at last he had a chance to read *the book,* which he'd been afraid to read until now.

The Theory and Practice of Oligarchic Collectivism

Winston felt a rush of excitement. With a title like that, it just had to be good.

Chapter One: Ignorance Is Strength

Since the dawn of man, there have been three principal varieties of humankind, each distinguishable by a distinct set of traits and characteristics: the idiots, the morons, and the bastards. . . .

Winston realized he'd be coming back to the first chapter later, so he skipped ahead to the third.

Chapter Three: War Is Peace

The splitting up of the world into three great superstates was a necessary step in the evolution of human social organization, and the existence of Oceania, Eurasia, and Eastasia has ensured a perpetual state of warfare. This makes it easier for the governments to suck, and to make life suck for their people, and to ensure that everything sucks for everyone forever.

Winston read the whole chapter, and his eyes glassed over and he nodded off twice. It certainly clarified how things sucked, but it only clarified; it didn't give him any information that he could really call new. Julia arrived and they had sex, then Winston said he'd read her the book.

He started with chapter one. He read how the current state of things had been arrived at, and how the classes were now kept in order, and how there could never be any more revolutions because there were no longer any unhappy people, because at the first signs of unhappiness people were taken out and shot. And on and on it went, and they both struggled to stay awake. Winston pressed on, sure that the information he was risking his life for was in there somewhere. Then finally, as the chapter seemed to be drawing to a close:

. . . Here we reach the central secret. As we have seen, the mystique of the Party, and above all of the Inner Party, depends upon Double-think. But deeper than this lies the original motive, the never-ques-tioned instinct that first led to the seizure of power and brought Doublethink, the Thought Police, continuous warfare, and all the other necessary paraphernalia into existence afterwards. What this motive really consists of, the core secret and meaning of it all, is . . .

Suddenly Winston noticed that Julia had fallen asleep. He put the book down, pulled the comforter over both of them, turned out the light, and lay awake in bed. What was the secret? Would he ever learn? What could it be? It tormented him. He had to know. He fell asleep.

Before he had a chance to look at the book the next morning, however, the apartment was invaded by Thought Police. Winston and Julia were arrested. The arresting officer was O'Brien, and it was clear that the illegal diary and foun-tain pen dealer had been the informant. It had all been a setup. Not very futuristic, but effective.

"This sucks," Julia said, and a few of the men beat the crap out of her.

"I can't believe you'd beat a woman like that," Winston said. "That sucks." Then they beat the crap out of him.

Winston woke up in jail. He had been badly beaten. He was very hungry. He was taken out and slapped around from time to time. Days went by; weeks, months, maybe even years. He kept getting beat up. Whatever he said or did, the Thought Police would come in at erratic intervals and beat him, or pull his teeth, or cut his tendons, or tickle him until he wet his pants. He confessed to everything. Still they beat him. He confessed to more, they beat him more.

Finally one day two guards came in and grabbed him, and O'Brien entered the cell. "I'm going to torture you until you realize that Big Brother loves you, and that you love Big Brother."

"Big Brother sucks," Winston said, and they tortured him again. O'Brien watched without saying anything. When they were done, and Winston lay only half-conscious in a crumpled, bloody, broken heap on the floor, O'Brien said, "Take him to Room 101."

In Room 101 he was strapped into a chair. O'Brien smiled wickedly and pressed a button. Music filled the room. It was the overture to *The Mikado*! O'Brien played the complete works of Gilbert and Sullivan over and over, sometimes singing along. At last, in the middle of "I Am the Very Model of a Modern Major General," Winston broke down. He could take no more. "Don't torture me," he cried, "torture Julia, kill her, I don't care, just leave me alone!"

"I was hoping you'd say that," said O'Brien. "You're free to go."

A few months later, while taking a limp around the lake, Winston bumped into Julia. She looked like a skeleton, her hair was falling out, her face was a purple potpourri of welts and bruises, and she had lost all her teeth. Worst of all, her breasts sagged.

"I betrayed you," Winston said.

"I betrayed you," Julia said right back.

"I'd betray you again," Winston said.

"I'd betray you first," Julia said.

"You suck," Winston said.

"You suck worse," Julia said.

They went their separate ways.

A few weeks after that Winston was sitting alone at a café drinking gin and reading the papers, as he did every afternoon. Once in a while he'd look up at the big poster, BIG BROTHER IS WATCHING YOU, and feel a certain reassurance. He didn't mind it so much anymore. It was sort of comforting to be watched. He wasn't an exhibitionist, but he liked the idea that someone was looking out for him. Suddenly all the telescreens began trumpeting an important announcement: major victory! Triumph over Eastasia in the most important and decisive battle of the long war! Big Brother was prevailing over the terrible hordes of the east! Victory, victory, victory! Winston found himself tapping his feet to the rhythm of the chant, found himself murmuring, "victory, victory, victory," found himself giddy and excited at the scope of Big Brother's victory. And suddenly he felt filled with warmth; realization poured over him like milk over corn flakes; he had finally conquered himself. The future didn't suck after all. He loved Big Brother.

Maybe love was too strong a word.

But he liked him. He really, really liked him.

—The End—

The Catcher in the Rye

by J. D. Salinger

(1951)

That's the whole trouble. You can't ever find a place that's nice and peaceful, because there isn't any. You may *think* there is, but once you get there, when you're not looking, somebody'll sneak up and write "Fuck you" right under your nose. Try it sometime. I think, even, if I ever die, and they stick me in a cemetery, and I have a tombstone and all, it'll say "Holden Caulfield" on it, and then what year I was born and what year I died, and then right under that it'll say "Fuck you." I'm positive, in fact.

There was so much History in the first half of the twentieth century that many writers chose to ignore it altogether, focusing instead on more personally relevant issues, such as the migratory habits of the ducks in New York's Central Park. J. D. Salinger was one such writer.

Salinger was a one-hit wonder. (He did write several other books, but these are of interest only to insomniacs and those with wobbly furniture.) The Catcher in the Rye was published in 1951, and Salinger subsequently hid himself away in the hills of Vermont, emerging from this self-imposed cloister only once, briefly, to serve as prime minister of Canada. For nearly half a century, The Catcher in the Rye has captured the imagination of the American teenager like no other book without pictures. Holden Caulfield, the hero and narrator of Salinger's slim classic, may be the finest portrait of twentieth-century American teenage angst bequeathed to posterity. Either him or Archie, it's hard to say.

You probably want to know all about my parents and how I grew up and all that crap, but you can go fuck yourself. I'm the one telling this crazy goddam story. My parents are morons, my kid brother Allie died of leukemia a couple of years ago, and my brother D.B. was this great writer but ended up moving to Hollywood to be a prostitute for the movies. The only one left worth a damn is my kid sister Phoebe. She's just ten, but she'd knock you out.

I'm in L.A. now, in this crazy goddam sanatorium that's

supposed to cure my T.B., but they won't let me out. Which is weird, when you think about it, because I haven't even coughed in about six months and I never heard of electroshock treatment for T.B. But don't get me started on this place. I want to tell you about all this madman stuff that happened last year around Christmas.

This winter I'm about to tell you about I was at Pencey Prep. My parents kept sending me to all these snobby boarding schools, and I don't know what I hated more: the goddam teachers, the goddam students, the goddam food, or the goddam circle jerks. You've probably seen old Pencey Prep's ads in all the magazines. They make it look like it's a bunch of swell guys playing polo and rugby and hunkering down in the library with big old books of French poetry or some damn thing. But what it really is, it's just a bunch of lousy goddam phonies from rich families doing each other up the butt. Believe me, I've been to four boarding schools. If there's one thing I can't stand, it's getting it up the butt. Especially by one of those goddam snobs in their Irish sweaters that their precious goddam grandmothers knit them. I mean, I feel just awful when I think about these guys' grandmothers. Here's this poor sweet old lady knitting away in some lonely little nursing home in New Jersey, thinking how her grandkid's gonna do the family proud by studying a bunch of crap about Yeats and Milton and Homer, and she hasn't got the slightest idea what he's up to in that sweater. It makes me want to cry, I'm not kidding.

I'm a terrific crier. You never saw anyone cry like me. I'll cry over just about anything. Sometimes I'll cry because the sky looks so goddam blue. Sometimes I'll cry because I see a pretty girl do some private thing, some little thing when she doesn't think anyone's watching, like biting a nail, or picking her nose, or doing a funny little twirly thing with her hair, or sucking a cucumber. I'm crazy that way, I really am.

I had this roommate, Stradlater. He was very popular with

girls, Stradlater was, but it was all an act. He came across like this real sincere prince of a guy, but he was a lousy slob. Not the ordinary kind of slob, not like old Ackley, but a slob in these very secret ways. He'd shave with this lousy rusty razor, and his combs always had all this hair stuck in them, and he never washed his butt plugs. He was very unhygienic. Girls never seemed to notice because they could never keep their goddam eyes off his crotch. I won't spoil his precious goddam secret, the phony bastard, but let's just say I never met a guy with so many goddam socks.

Then there was Ackley. Old Ackley was disgusting, I'm not kidding. He had this green shit all over his teeth, like *moss,* for Chrissakes, and there was always crud under his nails, and he had this awful breath, and his face was covered with open sores, and his whole chest and back were covered with these giant whiteheads that oozed gallons of yellowish pus. He was a prince, old Ackley was. I told him so.

To tell you the truth, I was glad to be thrown out of old Pencey.

The day I finally left I went to visit the only teacher I could stand, Mr. Spencer. He'd been out with the grippe so I had to visit him at his house, which wasn't on campus. Mr. Spencer was this crazy old guy who stuttered and drooled, but I always got a kick out of him. He had this wife, this skinny old broad with a flap of skin under her neck, like one of those birds with a flap of skin under its crazy neck. But her and the prof were just crazy about each other, and it just about broke my goddam heart. Lots of things'll break my heart like that. I've probably got the most broken-up heart you ever saw. I'm not kidding. And did I tell you I've got gray hairs? No kidding, all over one side of my head. It's from the experiments they conducted on me when I was a kid.

It was snowing like hell when I walked over to old Spencer's place. You could barely see ten feet in front of you, and every time you crossed the street you felt like you were about to be teleported into an alien spaceship and whisked off to another galaxy. That's just the kind of day it was.

If some stupid musician ever comes along and sings a lot of optimistic crap about peace and love and happiness, and makes millions of dollars writing a lot of crumby songs about how money doesn't mean anything, and stages a love-in for world peace, someone should kill the goddam phony bastard. Or if an actor ever becomes president. You've got to kill these phonies, it's the only way to stop them. Seriously. I'm talking to you. Yes, you. Kill. Kill. Kill.

Mrs. Spencer let me in and I could tell by the way she looked that she already knew they'd kicked me out of school. And there was old Mr. Spencer, sitting in this big maroon recliner. They had one of those awful little living rooms that old people never seem to mind, with those idiotic glass jars of herbs and blossoms and crap that are supposed to make the place smell nice but always end up smelling like some old couple's pathetic living room. The Spencers' living room also had some nasty bitter smell that made me wonder if Mrs. Spencer was a little behind on changing her old man's diaper.

Old people always have these awful-smelling bowel movements, and it depresses all hell out of me. I don't hold it against them *personally* or anything. I mean, it's funny about crap: we're all crapping all the time, but we hardly ever talk about it until we're so old there's nothing left to talk about. My grandmother, right before she died, you couldn't tell her enough about your bowel movements. She'd want to know if it was runny or mealy or a good solid stool. Was it clumpy? What color was it? Green? Brown? Black? Was there stuff in it? What kind of stuff? Did it all cling together in the bowl, or did it kind of crumble gradually? If you answered all her questions she could tell you everything you'd eaten in the last five days, what you'd been up to, whether you'd had a smoke, and who you'd voted for in the last election. If she could have smelled old Spencer's bittersweet little turds that day she probably could have predicted the time of his death to the minute. She was never wrong. I'm not kidding. She could have written a book about the stuff. That's the thing about turds, though: they're honest. There's no such thing as a phony turd.

Mr. Spencer offered me his wrinkled old liver-spotted hand and I shook it gently. I was afraid it'd crumble into powder if I squeezed too hard.

"Well, Holden, you've finally gone and done it, haven't you?"

Mrs. Spencer went off to make tea, or get some cookies, or refill the birdfeeder, or whatever the hell it is old broads do in the kitchen when their lousy old husbands start busting some kid's nuts.

"Yes, sir," I said. "I just came by to say good-bye."

He nodded but he didn't say anything. He pulled a folded-up piece of composition paper out of one of his robe pockets, and the minute I saw it I knew what it was. "I want to read you something," he said, and for a minute I thought maybe I could club him over the head with a baseball bat and get out of there before he started. I would have, but I didn't have a baseball bat. "I'm going to read you the essay you wrote for your midterm, Holden."

"I wish you wouldn't do that, sir."

" 'The Ancient Egyptians,' by Holden Caulfield, eleventh grade."

"I know why I failed, sir, I think—"

But the son of a bitch read my paper anyway:

The ancient Egyptians were these very backward people who piled a big bunch of rocks on top of each other into huge triangles. These so-called pyramids are still standing, although Egyptian civilization has long since disappeared off the face of the goddam earth.

Modern science does not understand how a bunch of backward ass peoples such as these alleged Egyptians could have done such a thing without the assistance of engineers from outer space, perhaps from a civilization which had developed advanced technology for piling rocks into triangles. Indeed, it may have been the very same outer space engineers who performed tests on me when I was child, thus making the one side of my head have gray hairs even though I am not yet of the age where it is considered normal to have a lot of gray hairs on your goddam head. We may never know.

Also they made mummies, and the mummies too have perplexed modern science for thousands of years.

P.S.: Mr. Spencer: I am sorry this is not a very good report on the Egyptians. I will never remember how to spell Tooton-fucking-common and it's not your goddam fault.

—HC

After he read it aloud he just looked at me like he was waiting for me to say something, or maybe he was waiting for his wife to come back into the room and say that tea was being served, or maybe he had just kind of blinked out for a minute like my grandfather used to before they removed the shrapnel. But I wasn't about to wait all day for him to finish giving me a load of crap. So I walked right up beside the chair and grabbed a handful of his lousy gray hair and slapped him a couple of times, then let myself out. He was speechless. Old people are never expecting you to hit them, that's why it's so effective when you do.

Anyway, that wasn't how I wanted to say good-bye to Pencey. Really I wanted to blow the whole crazy goddam place to bits. But the lousy bastards at the hardware store wouldn't sell me any dynamite, and I couldn't remember how to make a Molotov cocktail, so I finally just grabbed my goddam bag, put on my hunting cap, and left.

I took the train to New York and rented this really depressing hotel room on Times Square. I looked out the window and could see across the courtyard into this room on the other side of the hotel. There was this guy and this girl in there, and they were squirting mouthfuls of water on each other. I guess they thought it was sexy, I just thought it was stupid and depressing. I mean, you get a girl like that into one of these lousy goddam hotel rooms, some nice girl who's willing to let you take her to a crumby hotel like that, and who wants to squirt water on her? What I'd want to do is, I'd want to play checkers or something.

I got kind of lonely thinking about that. Not the kind of lonely where you want to go up on the roof with a rifle and start taking potshots at strangers, but the kind of lonely where you want to walk down the street holding a girl's hand and just goofing on silly stuff, like the faces homeless people make when you piss on them, or the different sounds a cat'll make depending how you kick him. I thought about calling my kid sister Phoebe, but then my parents probably would have answered the phone, so that was out. Finally I just pulled on my hunting cap and went out to this nightclub, The Lavender Room.

I danced with these three homely women from Seattle. They were insurance adjusters or something, and this was their big vacation. New York. Very Big Deal. They had seen Peter Lorre earlier that day. It was all they could talk about. I told them I was Peter Lorre's cousin and that I could probably get them introduced—if, that is, they wouldn't mind coming back to my room for a little action. They got all shocked and everything and stopped dancing. They got out of there in a flash. They left me with their goddam tab, which I thought was pretty presumptuous, so I grabbed their empties and chased them out into the street and threw the glasses at them. I caught one of them on the jaw, but it didn't look like I drew blood.

Then I got to thinking about Jane Gallagher, this girl I used to know, and how great it would be see her, and I came this close to calling her, but then I remembered that old Stradlater had already banged her earlier that night. (That was another one of the reasons I got the hell out of Pencey, only I didn't feel like getting into it before.) Anyway, old Jane was probably all lousy with crabs by now, and who the hell wants to play checkers with someone all lousy with crabs? Not me. So I went to this other club I used to like, Ernie's, in the Village. I took a cab. The cabby was this thick-necked slob, Horwitz. Probably one of the Elders of Zion driving a cab as cover. I asked old Horwitz what he thought happened to the ducks that hung around the pond in Central Park during the winter.

He smiled at me in the rearview—trying to gain my trust, the crafty bastard. "Never mind the ducks. What about the fish? What about them?"

"I don't know about the fish," I said. "I was wondering about the ducks."

"Ducks gotta eat the fish, right? Where're the fish, huh? Under the ice."

"I don't care about the fish, you Zionist bastard, I asked about the ducks. Stop trying to twist my words. I know what you're up to, I know what all you Elder Bastards of Zion are up to, with your brain implants, and your spies at the Vatican, and—"

He slammed on the brakes and threw me out. That's the problem with Jews, you can never really talk with them. They're so goddam touchy.

Well, old Ernie's was a wash, so I ended up heading back to the hotel after all. The elevator guy asked me if I was looking for some action.

"No, thanks," I said. "I'm flattered, I mean I'm flattered, but no thanks."

"I meant some action wid a broad, bright boy."

"Oh," I said. "Oh, sure, a broad. How much?"

"Five bucks a throw, fifteen all night."

"Sure," I said. "Sure, I'll take a throw." I gave him my room number.

"I'll send Sunny right up," he said, and he did.

Sunny showed up in a bright yellow dress. She wasn't so bad looking in the dress, but when she took it off she looked all pasty-white and she had all these awful bruises everywhere. She looked kind of bumpy, like a lousy mattress.

Suddenly I kind of lost interest. I mean I lost interest. Suddenly I felt real sad and lonely. I asked Sunny if she'd ever read *Leaves of Grass*.

"Leaves? You mean blades, right? It's blades of grass, not leaves. Leaves are on trees, grass is blades."

"No," I said. "*Leaves of Grass*, it's a book of poems."

"Poems, huh? Weird."

Then she got right to work, but I'll tell you something: looking down on her bobbing little head got me kind of blue, you know, kind of depressed. Here was this nice girl who I could have been playing checkers with. I kind of lost the urge.

Sunny shrugged and pulled her dress back on. "I still need the ten bucks," she said.

I grabbed my wallet off the bureau and handed her a five. "It was five," I said. "That was the price, five bucks."

Sunny shrugged. "You can explain it to Maurice," she said, and she left the room. A few minutes later there was a knock on my door. It was the elevator guy, Maurice. I let him in and stared at him defiantly.

"Five bucks, chief," he said.

"I gave her five," I said.

"Five more, chief."

I was feeling pretty tough. "Piss off," I said.

It only took Maurice about a minute to beat bloody hell out of me. It was sort of impressive, actually. I'm a pacifist myself, when I'm not too angry or drunk, but you had to admire the way old Maurice kicked my ass. There was nothing phony about it. It was a very sincere ass-kicking. Seriously. If I had to have my ass kicked again by anyone, it'd definitely be Maurice.

The next couple of days were pretty hard. I was kind of a maniac, if you want to know the truth. I kept calling these old girls I knew, these girls who I used to kind of like to horse around with, who I thought maybe wouldn't be such a big pain in my ass. I'd call them and meet them and we'd talk and stuff, but the thing is, sooner or later they were all a pain in the ass. Even Sally Hayes. I took her to Rockefeller Center and we ice-skated and all, but she wouldn't marry me or anything. That's the thing about girls, they never want to marry you if you're kicked out of boarding school.

One night I ended up pretty plastered and decided to go visit old Phoebe. I knew my parents were probably home and I wouldn't be able to see her, but I sort of didn't care anymore. I was pretty goddam drunk.

Luckily my parents weren't home, so I kind of snuck into Phoebe's room and just looked at her sleeping there for a minute. Phoebe knocks me out. I wish you could meet her. She's the most intelligent person I know. I looked around her room and flipped through her notebooks and checked out all her drawers and stuff, because I thought maybe someone might have hidden microphones or something in her room. People are always hiding microphones or something in your room.

Suddenly she woke up.

"Holden!"

"Sh!"

"What are you doing here? Mom said you wouldn't be here until Wednesday. Until *Wednesday,* she said. You got kicked out of school again, didn't you? Oh, Holden, Daddy's gonna kill you. Julie Grundermeyer's teaching me how to belch. You've been drinking. I get to play Benedict Arnold in our Christmas pageant Friday. Did you get my letter? You look so angry, Holden. You're always angry about things. You always hate everything."

Phoebe wakes up pretty quickly.

"I like plenty of things," I said.

"Name one," she said.

To tell you the truth, I couldn't really think of anything. "I should go," I said.

Phoebe looked like she was about to cry. "It's true, you hate everything, you even hate me. You can't even *imagine* something to like. What are you gonna do for a living, Holden? How are you gonna pay a mortgage? How are you gonna support a family? You've got to learn to handle responsibility."

"I'll get a job," I said. "I mean, I'll get a job. You know what I was thinking I could do was, was be that guy in the poem who stands at the edge of the cliff and keeps the kids from falling off."

"What are you talking about? How much did you drink? What poem?"

"You know: 'The Guy Who Stops Kids from Falling Off the Cliff.'"

"I never heard of it. Listen, Holden, you've got to wake up and fly straight. You're all paranoid and depressed. You might have an organic brain disorder or something. Anyway, it's late, and I'm just a little kid, so I need my sleep. Take the money out of my piggy bank and get out of here. Don't come home until Wednesday or Dad'll kill you."

That Phoebe. She just knocks me out.

I went from there over to the apartment of this old teacher of mine, Mr. Antolini. He was a pretty good guy. Him and his wife were still cleaning up from a dinner party or some damn thing. There were glasses and stuff all over.

Or maybe they didn't have a dinner party, maybe they just wanted me to think they'd been entertaining. You can never tell with people. Sometimes they want you to think they've been entertaining.

Mr. Antolini gave me this whole big speech about how I was a complete and total screw-up, and how I was beginning a free-fall into the abyss, and how if I didn't snap out of it I'd probably end up like one of those bitter old phony bastards I can't stand, or some kind of crazy assassin or something. It was one of those very corny speeches that was supposed to motivate me or something. I didn't feel like being motivated.

So I went over and spent the night on a bench in Grand Central, which was pretty depressing. The next morning I kind of wandered around for a while. I decided to head out west and pretend to be a deaf, dumb, blind quadriplegic. That way I wouldn't have to talk to anyone. I wouldn't have to deal with any phonies. It would just be me and my hunting cap. And what I'd do is, I'd set up land mines all around the outside of the house, so even if anyone tried to come bother me they'd get blown to hell. I'd let Phoebe visit me, and maybe D.B., but no one else. That's what I'd do.

I dropped a note at Phoebe's school telling her to meet me for lunch at the museum so I could say good-bye and give her all her dough back before I moved out west to be this deaf, dumb, blind quadriplegic with land mines and everything. While I was waiting for her I saw these two very young kids who were looking for the mummies.

"Hey, mister," the older one said, "you know where's the mummies?"

"Sure," I said. "Follow me. You know, the mummies are very interesting. They're about the most interesting goddam things in the museum. See, the ancient Egyptians made them in this way that has perplexed modern science for thousands of years. They also made pyramids out of these huge rocks, which was also very interesting." Suddenly I realized I was helping these kids out with a bunch of information I never thought mattered. They were pretty impressed. I mean, they were pretty impressed.

Eventually Phoebe showed up carrying this huge suitcase. She said she wanted to come out west with me. It was very clever psychology, so I decided that I wouldn't move out west after all. I decided instead that I'd let her wear my hunting cap and we'd go down to the carousel at the zoo so I could watch her go around and around and reach for the gold ring, since I knew that I wouldn't be able to wrap up the whole crazy week and wind up here in the hospital without a whole bunch of goddam symbols and everything.

People always want you to have a lot of goddam symbols and everything.

—The End—

The Old Man and the Sea

by Ernest Hemingway

(1952)

Imagine if each day a man must try to kill the moon, he thought. The moon runs away. But imagine if a man each day should have to try to kill the sun? We were born lucky, he thought.

After the First World War most of Western Civilization was extremely happy, principally because it was no longer being shot at. Americans in particular became so happy that liquor had to be outlawed to prevent them from becoming downright giddy. The strategy proved ineffective, and with the nation on the brink of utter exuberance there was no longer any choice but to have a Great Depression. This worked.

Europe, too, experienced great happiness in the 1920s, except for those countries that were unhappy, such as Germany, Italy, and Spain. It was eventually determined that people in those countries were unhappy because the trains were never on time, so they invented fascism to address this short-coming.

Having resolved the train schedules, however, fascists discovered that many people were still unhappy. This was found to be the result of socialism, and persons who failed to become happy were subsequently shot. This caused the Spanish Civil War, which was so successful it inspired World War II.

Against this backdrop of war and peace, happiness and unhappiness, drunkenness and sobriety, Ernest Hemingway matured as a writer. He drove an ambulance in the First World War, got drunk in Paris in the 1920s, and worked as a journalist in the Spanish Civil War. In his later years he spent a lot of time fishing in Cuba, learning what it meant to be a man.

The Old Man and the Sea *is the poor man's* Moby-Dick. *This is the tale of an old man ("The Old Man") named Santiago catching a big fish (not as big as Moby Dick, but pretty big just the same). It is written almost entirely in simple declarative sentences. Most of the words are short. Most importantly, like its longer predecessor, it makes a clever metaphor for just about anything. Intellectuals are quick to point out that Santiago is an anagram for "So, a giant!"—forgetting in their haste that anagram is itself an anagram for "a rag man."*

Hemingway was a handsome and robust heterosexual hero who never had the slightest doubts about his own masculinity. He wrote a lot of books about terse, unhappy, sexually unfulfilled men, then blew his brains out. Decades later, in 1999, he wrote one final book, and this galvanized his reputation forever: only a robust and heterosexual hero without the slightest doubts about his own masculinity could have written a book with his brains blown out.

He was an old man who fished alone in a skiff in the Gulf Stream and he had gone eighty-four days now without taking a fish. In the first forty days a boy had been with him. But after forty days without a fish or a proposal of marriage, the boy's parents had told him that the old man was now *salao*—completely fucked. They ordered him to sail with another boat, which caught three fish the first two days. It made the boy sad to see the old man come in each day with his empty skiff and he always went down to help him carry either the coiled lines or the harpoon and the gaff or the sail furled around the mast. He would help the old man carry them home, and they would talk.

The old man lived in a big cardboard box on the side of a hill—not a fancy cardboard box: the old man did not like things to be fancy. He laughed at the young men with their corrugation and their reinforced flaps. His was big enough to contain the rusty bucket he used as a chair, the heap of seaweed he used as a cot, and the aluminum milk crate he used as a table. Sometimes he felt the milk crate was too luxurious for a man of his own simple tastes, but in the right light its silvery matte finish was shiny like a fish, and he liked that. So he kept it, and hoped the spirit of his departed wife would forgive him his indulgence.

It was cramped in the box when the boy followed him in, but the old man did not mind. He liked to feel the boy's supple warmth press against him.

"Santiago," the boy said. "I could go with you again. The boat has made some money, I could come with you tomorrow." The old man had taught the boy to fish, and the boy loved him the way a young boy loves a man who teaches him how to fish.

"No," Santiago said, "you are with a lucky boat. Stay with them."

"But remember how you went eighty-seven days without a fish, and then we caught a fish every day for three weeks?"

"Those were good days," the old man said.

"Yes," said the boy.

"But they were different days."

"Yes."

Santiago sighed. "These are not bad days," he said, "but they are different from the good days."

"Yes," the boy said, "they are different."

"Different," the old man said.

"Yes," said the boy.

"But not bad," the old man said.

"No," said the boy.

"But not the same."

"No," the boy said, "not the same."

"Yes," said the old man.

"Yes what?" said the boy.

"Yes they are not the same," said the old man.

"No," said the boy. "No, yes, they are not."

The old man and the boy were silent.

"What will you have for dinner tonight?" the boy asked.

"Dirt and seaweed," the old man said. "It is a good meal, a man's meal. Why don't you eat with me?"

The boy saw through his pride. They went through this often. "I'm going to get some chili and rice and corn bread," the boy said. "More than I can eat. Would you like to share some?"

The old man shook his head. "Dirt and seaweed," he said. "This is all a fisherman needs."

"Yes," the boy said, "it is a good meal, but my mother is *loco* like a *pollo*. If I do not eat the chili and the rice and the corn bread she will become very upset, but it is too much for me to eat. If you help me eat it, I will be grateful."

The old man nodded. "Bring me this chili," he said. "And bring me this rice and this corn bread, and I will help you with your mother who is *loco* like a *pollo*."

So the boy left the box and came back later with some chili and rice and corn bread, which they ate.

When he had finished eating, the old man said, "We will talk of baseball now. The Yankees of New York cannot be beaten."

"I fear the Indians of Cleveland," said the boy.

"The Yankees of New York cannot lose," the old man said.

"I fear both the Tigers of Detroit and the Indians of Cleveland," the boy said.

"Think of the great DiMaggio," the old man said.

"The great DiMaggio still has the spur in the bone of his ankle," the boy said. "He cannot play today, or tomorrow, or perhaps the day after that, and perhaps there will even be days after that on which he will not be able to play, and that is why I also fear the Reds of Cincinnati, and even the White Sox of Chicago."

Santiago shook his head. "Eighty-four days without a fish. We should not talk of the grand leagues, even though it is a great and noble game in which there is much truth of what it means to be a man. We will speak no more of baseball. Let us talk about the marlins of Florida."

And so the man and the boy talked about fish and soon the old man fell asleep. The boy wrapped him in seaweed to keep him warm through the night and left him there.

That night the man dreamed of his youth, when he was young and not so old as he was now. He sailed the shores of

Africa and watched the lions playing on the shore at dusk. He loved the lions. Not the Lions of Detroit, but the lions of Africa, which were stronger and handsomer but could not play football worth a damn. One day he had seen a man charged by a lion; the man's wife tried to shoot the lion, but killed her husband instead. Santiago had thought to himself, "Either that woman is not a very good shot, or that woman is a very good shot."

He woke up and met the boy and they had a cup of coffee together, then the boy helped him rig the skiff and the old man sailed out alone.

"This is my eighty-fifth day since I have had a fish," he told the sea. "You have been very kind to me, and you have been very cruel to me. I loved the boy, and because of you I have lost him, and now I sail alone. Were you jealous? Did you want me for yourself?" Santiago still thought of the sea as *la mar,* a woman. A very big woman, made entirely out of water.

The sun rose and Santiago continued eastward. He had four lines trailing off the skiff, five if you counted the Bassmaster, all of them baited and trailing at different depths. The old man saw some birds circling a little north of him; he aimed the boat up toward them. Within moments he had caught a ten-pound albacore tuna. It would make good bait.

"The birds have been lucky for me," he said. "Although it is maybe not so much luck, to catch a ten-pound tuna in these waters."

The old man couldn't remember when he had started talking to himself, or why he spoke to himself in awkward English rather than his native Spanish. It seemed like he had always been talking to himself, and he had never enjoyed the conversation.

"I would like for once not to talk to a fool," he said. Then he became insulted.

"Who are you calling fool?" he said.

The Old Man and the Sea • 205

• • •

His argument was interrupted by a tug at the deepest line, and it was a strong pull. "It is a big fish," the old man said, "a very big fish. A really big, really strong fish." It pulled him to the east. It pulled him for hours. The sun went down, and there was only the dim glow of Havana in the west, and soon that, too was gone, and it was nothing but darkness. It was just him and the fish, the really big, really strong fish, and Santiago loved him.

"You are a beautiful fish," he said, "and I love and respect you because you are a strong fish and you are doing what you must to beat me. But as much as I love and respect you, I will beat you and I will kill you, because that is what I must do. Tonight it is only you and me, fish. It is your strength against my intelligence. It is a veritable potpourri of metaphor, every nuance of which is fraught with meaning."

The fish continued east as the moon rose, and the old man could not believe the strength of the fish. He wished he could see it. He wished he knew its name and could talk to it in its little fishy language. "Hello, fish," he would say. "Hello, Santiago," the fish would say. "You've certainly pulled me a long way out," the old man would say. "You've certainly demonstrated incredible patience and endurance," the fish would say. And then they would hug, and tears would stream down their cheeks, for they would both have learned something about being a man. Or something about being a fish. Either way.

Not long after sunrise a sudden jerk of the line smashed him against the inside part of the boat that's underneath the edge of the side but in front of where the mast goes, and it hurt his left hand terribly. It was bleeding and cramped, and clenched itself into a claw. "I will need that hand to catch this fish," the old man said, so he ate the tuna raw. He was angry that he had no wasabi or soy sauce on the skiff.

The nutrients from the tuna helped his hand, and by noon

it was uncramped, unclenched, unclawed. It was good tim-
ing, because just then the fish finally broke the surface, its
broad silvery back arching above the sparkling gray sea.

"Fish," the old man said, "my beautiful fish!" It was a marlin. "And now the struggle begins!" the old man said. He was
not a religious man, but he prayed for the strength to land
this fish. "I am an old man and have been eighty-five days
without a fish," he said. "Let me have this fish and I will say a
hundred Hail Marys. No, that's too much: fifty. No, it isn't the
number of prayers but the quality of prayer: I'll give you one
Hail Mary and whatever I can remember of the Pater Noster." He couldn't remember any of the Pater Noster, so he
was glad he was not religious.

The fish had gone down again, and continued pulling him
east.

"I wonder if I have done well," the old man said. "I wonder if the great DiMaggio would approve. He has played
some games with that spur of the bone of his ankle, and he
has done well in some of them. I wonder what a spur of the
bone of an ankle is. I wonder if it is as bad as my pain, as the
soul-crushing poverty I endure every day or the terrible
obscurity under which I toil without a thought to anything
but earning an honest meal."

And the afternoon became the evening, and the sun finally set behind him. And it was the night of the second day. The
old man caught a dolphin with one of the other lines and
gutted it with his good hand, since the other was cramping
again. In the belly of the dolphin were two flying fish. He cut
the head off one and ate it, and felt its strength go through
him. "Now I know I can beat this fish," he said. He hadn't
finished chewing and it was not attractive to see the chewed-
up fish in his mouth as he spoke.

Later it was late at night, and the old man knew he would
have to sleep. He squared himself against the mast and closed
his eyes and let sleep come to him. He dreamed of lions play-

ing on the African shores at dusk. This was his recurring dream, that's important. Don't forget about those lions.

He awoke with a start to the fish jumping again; again the broad silver back arched over the shimmering water. The sun had risen. It was time for the final struggle. His left hand was numb again, cramped into a claw, and he ate the second flying fish to gain some strength. Now he set to work, taking in line as the fish begin his despairing circles. It was grueling, monotonous work, and it took four hours, but at last the old man had drawn the fish within harpooning distance. He raised his harpoon and aimed for the fish's heart. "Now from hell's heart I stab at thee," he said. "For hate's sake, with my dying breath I spit at thee . . ."

No, that wasn't him. The old man just said *"aiyee!"* and loosed the harpoon, and watched as the fish rolled on its side, dead, its strength streaming out in a thin ribbon of blood that billowed into a great dark cloud in the water.

The old man reeled him in, hauled him alongside the skiff, and wondered how to get him into the boat.

"You are a big fish," he said, "and it is a small boat. You are much too big to enjoy the sail back with me here in the boat, and you are even too big for me to tow you in. You will have to ride shotgun." And so the old man set about tying the fish fast to the side of the boat.

Down in the cold dark depths of the sea, a lonely old mako shark swam about, hungry, weary, friendless. He had been eighty-four days without a kill, the first forty of them with a pilot fish. After forty days, however, the pilot fish's parents had come along and told the pilot fish to prowl with a better shark, and so the old mako had eaten all three of them. That had helped. But it had been another forty-five days since then.

Out of nowhere a delicious scent caught his attention. "I know that scent," he thought. "It is the scent of marlin. I have been many days without a fish, and a marlin could get me through the winter." But as mysteriously as it had come, the scent vanished. The old shark swum slowly, or swam slowly, sniffing. He caught the scent again and swam toward it, then lost it and swum aimlessly again. And then the scent came again, and he lost it again. This happened several times. The shark did not lose hope, because the scent seemed stronger every time he caught it. At last he caught it and it remained with him. He was able to follow it westward, and it became stronger with every league.

"Ah, marlin," he said, "you have swimmed well, considering how much blood you have lost, and I love and respect you, but now I must catch you and eat you, for that is my nature." Far ahead and far above him, he finally made out the swollen form of the marlin—and what luck! It was swimming alongside another, fatter marlin.

The old mako judged the distance between himself and the marlins, the speed at which they were traveling, and the best course of interception, and then moved in for the kill. He rose to the surface and felt the warm afternoon air on his exposed dorsal fin as he accelerated toward the marlin. At last he lunged forward and got his jaws around the base of the marlin's tail. It was good marlin, fresh, meaty. The old mako knew nothing after the taste of the marlin, for a harpoon had struck straight into his brain and ended his thinking even before he was dead.

The old man lost his harpoon on the first shark, and he tied his knife to the end of an oar to give himself a weapon against the next. Eventually they came, two shovelnose sharks, and although he was able to kill them both, they got more meat off the marlin and he broke the blade of his knife on the second of them. Not long after sunset the marlin was attacked by two more shovelnoses. He clubbed them senseless, exhausting what was left of his strength and losing the second oar in the process. A half hour later the marlin was beset by a mako, two shovelnoses, a hammerhead, and a phillipshead, and the old man stuck out his tongue and called them names. They made short work of what was left of the marlin; as they swam off, the old man was left with only the marlin's head, spine, and tail.

"You were a great fish," he said sadly, "a fish like perhaps no other. And now you are only a head, a spine, and a tail. And I was once a fisherman, a fisherman like perhaps no other, and now I am just an old man. I would call it a draw, except that I still have my internal organs."

It was very late when the old man guided the skiff onto the shore. He barely had energy enough to take down the mast and furl the sail; he left the coiled lines behind him and dragged the mast back toward his simple cardboard box on the hill. He had to stop and rest several times. Finally he was home, and he did not even take off his pants before he collapsed onto the fine bed of seaweed and fell into a deep, deep sleep.

The boy looked in on him first thing in the morning and wept when he saw the old man's hands. He ran down to the beach and saw a crowd gathered around the old man's boat. People were admiring the skeleton of the great marlin. "He is a good fisherman," he heard some people saying, "but he must have been very hungry."

The boy looked in on the old man again before setting out to sail that day. The old man appeared to be sleeping comfortably. He was. For in his dreams he was watching lions at play on the African shore at dusk, sipping a margarita with his friend the marlin, and his other friend the old mako shark, and they were all three drunk and laughing as the great DiMaggio stepped up to the plate.

—The End—

On the Road

by Jack Kerouac

(1957)

They rushed down the street together, digging everything in the early way they had, which later became so much sadder and perceptive and blank. But then they danced down the streets like dingledodies, and I shambled after as I've been doing all my life after people who interest me, because the only people for me are the mad ones, the ones who are mad to live, mad to talk, mad to be saved, desirous of everything at the same time, the ones who never yawn or say a commonplace thing, but burn, burn, burn like fabulous yellow roman candles exploding like spiders across the stars and in the middle you see the blue centerlight pop and everybody goes "Awww!"

At the end of the Second World War, America dropped two atomic bombs on Japan. Each bomb killed so many people in the blink of an eye, and made the world so safe for peace-loving democracies, that the nation began feeling pretty good about things and forgot all about being Depressed, etc. This caused the Hula-Hoop, the soda fountain, and Annette Funicello. Not everyone could master the Hula-Hoop, however, and the alienation experienced by those who couldn't resulted in the development of an American counterculture.

Scoffing at the traditional values of mainstream America, the counterculturalists experimented with bold new ideas. They forsook the established middle-class pleasures, such as wine, women, and song, in favor of radical new ones, such as sex, drugs, and rock 'n' roll.

A child of the Depression and a veteran of the Second World War, Jack Kerouac was torn between these competing value systems, and he roamed the country aimlessly in search of grammar and punctuation. The adventures described in On the Road *were based loosely on his real-life travels with the infamous Ken Kesey and his band of Merry Pranksters, whose insatiable appetite for borscht led Kerouac to dub them "The Beet Generation."*

I met Dean not long after my wife and I broke up, when I was feeling pretty weary and everything seemed kind of dead, and with the coming of Dean began the part of my life that you might call my life on the road, or, more accurately, my life spent living with my aunt in Paterson, New Jersey, with sporadic low-budget trips to visit friends in other cities, punctuated by adventures in those cities that weren't quite adventures so much as the same kind of human foolishness that we all must go through, the sad American indigo-evening foolishness of laughter and tears, and lust, and general goofing, and Dean was of course the greatest goof of them all, having come to my attention first through a series of letters he'd written to my friend Chad King inquiring about things like Nietzsche and Goethe and Kierkegaard and all the other great French philosophers, about whom Dean of course knew nothing, but about whom he wanted to know everything, because even though Dean never understood the complicated reasoning of philosophy, still he always knew that if he got the words down he could probably bang some of those hot college chicks, who really weren't normally his type, Dean preferring the shrill, mad, hysterical women like Marylou, his wife, little mad Marylou, who was beautiful and small and precious like a porcelain figurine, except that a porcelain figurine wouldn't be much fun in bed and to hear Dean and Marylou go at it in their coldwater west side flat you just knew that if she'd been made of porcelain she'd have been a heap of busted fragments on their tired, sooty floor, which happened to be the very floor on which I stood the first time I met Dean Moriarty, and from the first moment I knew him I knew he would be my saint, my patron saint of madness, and although I did end up following Dean for a number of years, from one side of this big sprawling country that's all wet on both ends and flat in the middle with bumpy parts between the wet sides and the flat middle, to the other, and though I tried to get to the middle of Dean, to the center of his sweet child's soul, his crazy larcenist's soul, his great goofy bigamist's child-abandoning soul, I never really succeeded because I hadn't learned something yet, and what I hadn't learned was what I had been trying to learn from that first long trip on, that trip he persuaded me to take after Marylou failed to be truly free and open and exuberant enough to clean up and have breakfast ready in the morning and therefore proved that she was not a very suitable wife, but a whore, driving Dean to leave her and come to stay with me at my aunt's, that trip, that first trip when I walked away from the manuscript of my novel and left my aunt's house in New Jersey and gathered up a few things in a duffel bag and took all the veteran's benefits money I'd been saving up and dropped out of Columbia and started off in search of the American night, and the American day, and even the American midafternoon, and some hard American truth buried under all the sticky-sweet gooey layers of American madness that were coating the country in those days just a few years after the war when everything seemed possible and every little circumstance seemed to be leading a straight line to something good and redeeming but ended up just to be a big one-way sign pointing to a big hole in the ground that eventually opened up and swallowed everything good and innocent we had, or maybe not quite as bad as all that, but which certainly devoured all our goodness and innocence, because whatever anyone says we were good, mostly, and innocent, usually, even though it's easy to look back and say that we were stealing a lot of stuff, especially cars, and getting women pregnant and running away from them, and sometimes marrying one chick before we were done with another, but it wasn't any lack of goodness or innocence, it was the frantic driving thump-thump-thump of Dean's maniacal pace that he set for us, and that we all followed, which is why when we came to that bridge and he said jump we all looked at each other and then jumped just because he'd said to, and our mothers be damned, and you can't hold it against him that he didn't jump himself because that wasn't Dean, Dean had to show us something about Dean, we had to learn that he was easily distracted, and this was something I learned, as I was saying, on that first trip, when I got out of New Jersey and took a bus to Chicago and was blown away by that gone old city by the lake, Chicago, that city with all those buildings and houses and stores and roads, Chicago, with all those peo-ple on sidewalks and crossing the street and sitting in their living rooms, Chicago, with the cars on the roads, some of them driving fast, some driving slower, some parked, and made my way to all the great centers of bop, and the great old sweaty negroes could blow in those days, and I caught all the great gone heroes of the whole bop scene, and I heard them blowing down in the Loop and up on North Clark and all over the whole great crazy city, and then I remembered I wasn't in Chicago to dig Chicago, but to get to Denver, to that city in the mountains, way the heck up there above sea level, where even now, as I hitched my way west, through Rock Island and Davenport, the Mississippi laying in between them like a mighty river between two banks, the great Mississippi, the big river, full of water, flowing along from north to south, passing places as it went, and then hitched further west across the great golden cornland of Iowa and Nebraska, or actually green cornland, since the corn was still green at that point, because the husks and stalks aren't golden, that's the corn, even now Dean and Carlo Marx and Chad King and Roland Johnson and Ed Rawlins, and his hot kid sister Beaver Rawlins, all of them were hav-ing great kicks without me, were sneaking out of their par-ents' houses at night and digging the great gone scene of Denver, all of them except Dean, who had no parents, and maybe that was what made him different from the rest of us, the fact that his father was a bum and used to roam around Larimer Street and Dean had been begging him out of jails for as long as he could remember, and had even run street gangs in Denver, and knew all the tricksters and hipsters of Larimer Street, and even the young men with huge bulging biceps, the snowy Adonises of the side-burned west, would step out of Dean's way when he came screaming through their scene in that way he had back then, shouting "yes yes yes!" to everything, for that was his mantra, it was Dean's HOLY YES—or maybe his WHOLLY YES, or even his HOLEY YES, he never spelled it out so it's hard to know and I'm not about to track him down and ask him now—and they understood that, or maybe they didn't understand that, in fact I'm almost certain they didn't, because they were just muscle-heads after all, and really what is sadder or emptier than the big-toothed smile of a Denver musclehead, except maybe the tragic old alcoholic riding in the back of the pickup truck that was driving me and a bunch of other wandering souls, with names like Montana Slim, Mississippi Gene, Delaware Dan, Rhode Island Roderick, across Nebraska and now into Wyoming, yes, that tragic old drunk who stood up to piss and couldn't stand up straight and lost control and fell over and pissed all over himself in the back of the truck, and didn't even seem to mind, or even notice—yes, yes, that was probably sadder, and it was also sad the way the other crazy lost souls in the back of that truck with me were all staring out at the bottomless American night with me, the sky open-ing up like a great big sunroof and revealing more and more how small you are, and everything looming up in the dis-tance and gradually getting bigger and bigger until you pass it and then you watch it get smaller and smaller until the horizon swallows it up, and that was how I looked back at Denver after I'd had my few days of kicks there, because the kicks weren't great there, because there'd been a falling out, because Dean and Carlo were in some kind of war with Roland Johnson and Chad King and the Rawlinses and all the rest of the gang, or maybe it was that they were all in a war with Dean and Carlo, I never figured that one out exactly, but people had taken sides, and feelings had been hurt, and Dean was already even back then going back and forth between Marylou and a new girl he'd fallen in love with, Camille, and he'd go from one to the other, actually nailing them more than once, then dashing out while they slept, spending all the additional time he could with Carlo, and they would sit on the bed in Carlo's little cave of an apartment facing one another and trying to get into the truth of their every conversation, tracing every thread of every word that passed between them back to its source: this was a passion of Dean's, he wanted to get to the truth, he wanted IT, he wanted to understand time, to know time, and he thought he did, and he thought that by following him we all would, but it seemed kind of vague to me, and Dean and Carlo let me watch while they sat opposite one another on the bed and tried to get clear with each other on absolutely everything that had happened between them from day one, and Dean was saying, "yes, yes, yes, and when we were walking by the mailbox a few minutes later and you exhaled, I said—" and Carlo interrupted him and said, "I wasn't exhaling I was inhaling," and Dean said that then he'd obviously completely misinterpreted his breathing rhythms at that moment and perhaps that was why he'd ended up scratching his ear a few moments later, and then Carlo said no, he hadn't scratched his ear, he'd scratched his chin, and Dean suddenly remembered this, and the revelation flowed through him, and again he exclaimed in the way he had then, and later, too, "yes, yes, ahem, yes, I see, and that's—yes, now I understand, I see it all—yes," and Carlo said "yes," and Dean said "yes," and I said, "for God's sake I'm trying to sleep," but they weren't tired even though by now the sun was up, the fabulous Denver sun that rose like a big red round thing over Kansas, and anyway I was running out of money and needed to hook up with old Remi Boncoeur, an old friend of mine from my service days,

218 • Greg Nagan

who was living in some godawful trailer on a military base outside of Frisco, so when I finally set out for Frisco, as I was saying, I looked behind me and saw the sun setting behind the great Rocky Mountains, which were big and rocky, only now that I think of it the sun probably wasn't setting behind them, but rising, because I was going west and leaving the mountains behind in the east, the sprawling messy gray east, and onward I lunged toward the Pacific, toward the end of the continent, toward the place where if you wanted to go further you couldn't because, you know, no more land, and I got there and there was a note on the locked door of Remi's trailer saying, "Come on in, Sal, if the door's locked you can climb through the window," and I probably should have told you my name by now, only there was so much to tell you that I couldn't justify interrupting, but for future reference my name is Sal Paradise, so when I saw that sign on the door I climbed on in and there was Remi in bed with some gorgeous little blonde I fell in love with right away named Lee Ann, and boy I would have loved to make Lee Ann, and there was one time when the three of us rowed out to an old abandoned ship in the middle of the harbor and I was up on the bridge and Lee Ann was laying out on the deck in the raw, and all I could think was how great it would be to take a diving leap right into her, and I later told Dean about that thought, and he laughed in that way he had then, "ah-hee-hee-hee-hee-HAW," and he said I should have, and I will probably always regret that I didn't, even though I know, as Dean surely also knew, that such a thing wasn't possible, and that probably if I had tried it I would have crushed her to death and broken at least a few of my own bones, so it was just as well that I hadn't, but Dean didn't understand this, Dean didn't understand precautions, because if you let precautions loom over everything you'd never get anything done, you wouldn't know time, you wouldn't find IT, and you'd certainly never eat Chinese food, but on the other hand I'm not sure if I was learning to know time or finding IT by watching Remi beat Lee Ann, or by helping Remi steal stuff from the canteen every night, and I sure didn't enjoy the night watchman job Remi got me where we had to walk around with guns and tell people to keep it down in there, and so finally I got wise, I got out of there, I left Frisco and hitched my way south, or tried to, until I got tired of hitching again, and went into the bus terminal in Sacramento, which was a pretty vague and crazy place, and bought a ticket for LA because I thought I should see LA before heading back to New York, and there on the bus I met this beautiful Mexican girl named Terry, and she had left her awful husband and was going to start life over, and we started talking in the bus and ended up shacking up together in LA and then starting a life together and I lived with her in a tent and picked cotton for a while and it was a crude little life but we were awfully in love and she couldn't have enough sex, but then her kid showed up, and it was complicated with her family, and it was time for me to go back to New York, and I went back, and I finished and sold my novel, and then Dean showed up again and I followed him off on another trip around the country, only this time we went a different way, and we spent some time down around New Orleans with an old friend who was pretty gone on heroin and whose wife was out of her mind on methamphetamines, and we did some stuff there, also crazy stuff, and then we went through Denver, and out to Frisco again, I think, unless we went somewhere else, and then back to New York, and this time I stayed awhile, and by now my aunt was moving to Long Island, and I lived there awhile and made some money and decided that I needed to take one more trip to wrap things up as far I was concerned and so I gathered up my money and I went out to Frisco and rescued Dean from Marylou who'd been having his children, and actually I tried making Marylou myself, and I did, but that was before she'd had a kid, and there was Inez by now, too, she'd had a kid, she was in New York, but it was Camille in Denver I had to rescue Dean from this time, I think, if I remember, and I grabbed Dean and we went out and dug the serious craziness of some great jazz hipsters and Dean was sweating and kept running out and stealing cars and then finally almost got caught so we had to sneak out of Denver like criminals, which in fact I suppose we technically were, and then we got a car and a guy named Stan and drove down to Mexico, down to plunder the bottom of the continent, that narrowed and trickled down toward Panama, stopping only once before Mexico City, in some high plateau town where we spent too much of our money on some grass and some whores and some drinks and then finally were in Mexico City, and I got real sick and Stan disappeared and Dean came and visited me in the hospital and said through his sweat, in that lunatic way he had then, said that he'd finally wrapped up the divorce with Camille which meant he could acknowledge the marriage with Marylou and therefore divorce her and move in with Inez, unless he wanted to leave Inez to divorce Marylou and marry Camille, and what he wanted to do with all those children I didn't know, and I didn't ask, because there was no need to ask, because I understood and Dean understood and there he left me, abandoned me in a Mexico City hospital, and you can bet your ass I still think of Dean Moriarty, you can bet your ass I still think of that wandering son-of-a-bitch, you can bet everything you've got I think of Dean Moriarty.

—The End—

Acknowledgments

In the interests of full disclosure, I'd like to acknowledge that I always skip other authors' acknowledgments and don't expect that many people will read mine. But I've received so much help, support, guidance, and advice in writing this book that, given my luck, the only people who'll read these acknowledgments are those whose support I've somehow overlooked. I beg their forgiveness. I am deeply indebted to my parents for having and raising me instead of some other person, and to Trine for all her patience. I'd also like to express my thanks and appreciation to Garrison Keillor; Christine Tschida; Rob Knowles; Gene and Debbie Lee; Howard Yoon; Lisa Miyako; Tony Millionaire; my favorite ex-wife, Allison Cain; Heather Donaldson; Sheldon Patinkin; Kenneth Northcott; Chris and Paul Peditto; Nick Digilio; and everyone at Simon's Tavern (in the heart of Andersonville) who was kind enough to read through the rough drafts even when I stopped buying them shots. And special thanks to Denise Roy and everyone else at Simon & Schuster for making the publication of my first book such a pleasure, including Steve Messina, production editing genius.

About the Author

In ninth grade, Greg Nagan was struck in the head by a shotput. He failed out of math and science in his junior year of high school. After attending several colleges and changing majors forty-three times over seven years before obtaining a degree, Mr. Nagan was at last well prepared to embark upon a career of changing careers. He has since worked in politics, public affairs, managed care, watermelon packaging, theatrical production, printing press operation, cooking, perfume sales, and government cheese distribution. He cofounded the critically acclaimed theatrical group igLoo in Chicago in 1985 and the international award-winning theater company Studio 108 in 1992. His comedies have appeared on stages throughout Chicago and his material has been heard on *A Prairie Home Companion* with Garrison Keillor. After a year of writing short skits for the show, his "Six-Minute *Iliad*" was broadcast on *APHC* in October 1996, followed in short order by other travesties of literature that ultimately inspired this book. He has no criminal record. His papers are in order.